Cliff Parker was born in Manchester in 1932 and
first saw the light of day in 1953 when he was
invited down to Aldershot to join the Virgin
Soldiers. His interest in fishing began when his
father took him down to the canal to learn to
swim. He fondly recalls those early struggles—
trying to get back to the surface with a brick in
each pocket. He lives now at Amersham in the
Chiltern Hills with his wife, two children and a cat
called Jemima who is not quite right in the head.
Parker is a man of many parts. Few of them
working. When he gave up his early ambition to be
a chicken farmer, Parker wandered into
journalism. He's still trying to find his way out.

The Fishing Handbook to End All Fishing Handbooks

CLIFF PARKER

Illustrations by Derek Alder

SPHERE BOOKS LIMITED
30–32 Gray's Inn Road, London WC1X 8JL

First published in Great Britain by
Wolfe Publishing Limited 1972
Copyright © Cliff Parker 1972, 1982
Published by Sphere Books Ltd 1982

Z 799.120207
JM 5/5/83
1.50

Set in 10/11 Compugraphic Baskerville

Printed and bound in Great Britain by
Cox & Wyman Ltd, Reading

Contents

CHAPTER ONE

The Lure Of Fishing

The open-air life beckons every one of us whose days are spent in the fumes and noise, smell and smoke, of the big city. Angling takes us away from it all to the canal bank. There in the restful shade of the cooling towers we can settle down in peace, inhaling the breeze-borne scent of the rubber factory, to watch the sunlight playing on the scuds of detergent foam. We are disturbed only by passing coal barges, towpath cyclists, bovver boys, dogs whose attentions leave the groundbait soggy, courting couples and solitary men in John Lennon spectacles and long raincoats.

Here is where we sublimate our shallowly-buried hunting instincts, where we rip aside the thin veil of civilisation from our primeval urges and give a blood-curdling howl of victory as we reel a two-ounce gudgeon to the bank.

Here is where we can study the wildlife of water and bank. Where we can watch the rats sorting through the rubbish in the disused boatyard. Where we can observe exotic sparrows and pigeons pecking at discarded crusts. Where a solitary seagull makes lonely circles in the sky, utters his call of a soul in torment, and delivers a message accurately into our open packet of sandwiches. Here we can admire the grace of passing swans, sailing like proud white ships to investigate our hookbait, responding with aristocrat's dignity to a swift prod with the landing net.

Here is where we can muse on the symbolism of the fishing rod. With it, a man is no longer limited in reach

Here is where we can muse on the symbolism of the fishing rod . . .

to the length of his arm. He is a man with a spear, with a finger fifteen feet long, from the end of which he can cast a bait to explore regions forty, fifty, sixty feet and more away.

With the rod and its gossamer line he is able to penetrate a foreign and still largely unknown element. As the bait sinks and drifts across the bottom, the angler is in contact with the hidden mysteries below the surface: with the rusting bicycle wheels, with old sewing machines, pram frames, mattresses and dead cats in weighted sacks.

With a rod the angler is able to explore at close quarters the mysteries of the upper air. As he climbs a tree to untangle his line, he becomes aware of a whole new world of caterpillars, spiders, earwigs, beetles, dusty leaves and branches too delicate to bear his weight.

With a rod he can muse upon the Freudian interpretation of it as a phallic symbol, and suddenly enter a whole new dimension of hitherto impossible conquests and delights. With a little further thought, however, he realises that with a sixteen-foot match rod his troubles would only just have begun.

With a rod he is the provider. Were our whole civilisation to disappear, he would be able still to feed his family. Providing he had an inexhaustible supply of hooks, floats, line, reels, rings, weights, and that his family were small enough to subsist on a daily diet of two gudgeon, four stunted roach and a one-eyed perch.

By the waterside, the mind of the angler is free to roam, untrammelled, over all the little unimportant things that crowd him on a normal working day. He has time to think about whether the bank manager *really* meant what he said in that last letter; whether the big end in the car *will* stand up for another six months; whether the dry rot in the loft *will* stop spreading; whether his redundancy notice *will* be coming through now that the firm's been taken over; whether the boss *has* forgiven him for what happened at the office party. He is free to consider all these petty problems objectively and at length. And to finish up as a gibbering wreck.

A day by the water is a great re-creator, a great

refresher, a great rejuvenator. It is always possible to spot the weekend angler back at work on a Monday morning. He has spent a healthy Sunday sitting through the usual mixture of freezing mist, intermittent drizzle, a couple of heavy showers and a persistent north east wind. And while everybody else is wandering around bleary-eyed and dull-witted, suffering from Monday morning blues, the angler is huddled purposefully over the radiator. Coughing.

In Britain alone there are about three million registered anglers. This excludes those who do not belong to clubs, those who borrow their mates' tickets, those who use last year's tickets and those whose hearing and sight are such as to render tickets unnecessary.

Most of them are men or boys. Though the past decade has shown a marked increase in the number of women anglers, the men still outnumber them by hundreds to one.

Why do they do it? What atavistic instinct takes them back, week after week, year after year, in all weathers, to the calm of the waterside?

The statistical section of *The Fishing Handbook to End All Fishing Handbooks* conducted a nationwide survey to find the answers. First analysis appeared to show that 98.5 per cent of the men went fishing to get away from their wives, but this was put down to a circuit fault in the computer and the fact that the programmer had been at the meths again. Pending a circuit check and re-programming, it might be of interest to examine the text of some of the interviews from the survey, and to follow them with the opinions of our resident psychiatrist.

First, to present the views of the younger generation, *John Paul George Ringo Slatterwick, aged 9, of Cable Street Mews, Bethnal Green:*

'I likes goin' fishin' 'cos me an' me bruvver can get lots of maggots an' worms an' fings an' mess abaht wiv 'em for a coupla days, puttin' 'em in our sister's cornflakes an' Dad's tea an' that. We genly puts 'em in Dad's tea when we're ready to go fishin' so that by the time 'e's spit 'em all aht an' unbuckled 'is belt, we're arfway dahn the street, ain't we?

'Then we flicks a few maggots at old darlins on the bus until we gets chucked orf, an' that saves us our fare, dunnit?

'We fishes near the power station where it says "Keep Aht" an' that. We climbs froo the bit where it says "Danger—High Tension Cables" an' that, then climbs over the wall wiv the broken glarss on the top, parst the notice abaht "No Unauforised Personnel" an' that, an' then we gets to the canal near the notice abaht no fishin' allowed an' that.

'Then we 'as a smashin' time stickin' the maggots and fings on the 'ooks an' watching' 'em wriggle an' that, an' then we fishes for a bit. If we don't catch nuffin', we frow stones an' that, an' genly me an' me bruvver 'as a bit of aggro an' I chuck 'im in the water 'cos 'e's smaller than me, innee?

'Genly some old geezer wiv a peaked cap turns up an' tells us to scarper. If 'e can't run so fast we tell 'im ter get knotted an' frow fings at 'im. 'E clears orf, dunnee, an' comes back wiv a noddy an' then we reely do scarper.

'When we gits back 'ome we're OK if Dad's gorn rahnd the boozer. If 'e's still in we cops it fer the maggots in 'is tea. Then Mum tries to stop 'im bashin' us an' 'e gives 'er a bunch o' fives, dunnee? Then they both go rahnd the boozer an' we can put the rest of the maggots in our sis's tights while she's gettin' ready to go dahn the Disco.

'I like fishin'.'

Our Resident Psychiatrist reports:

'Master Slatterwick's reactions are typical of those of his age and generation who find themselves growing up in an environment of economic and cultural deprivation.

'His little japes with the maggots help to establish healthy relationships within the family group, bringing him into close physical and emotional contact with his parents, who otherwise might tend to overlook his basic need for attention. In extending the joke to his sister he is putting up a subconscious defence against the underlying urge to an incestuous relationship.

'The antics on the bus, the trespassing on forbidden—possibly even dangerous—ground, and the final confrontation with the forces of law and order show a natural reaction against conformity, organised society, and the repressive agents of authority.

'The apparently sadistic interest in the impaling of the maggots indicates a lively appreciation of the delicacy of structure and complicated reflexes of even the lowest of living organisms, and bodes well for his future studies in fields such as biology, biochemistry, penal reform or any of the associated sciences.

'His tussle with his brother by the waterside and the subsequent ducking of his brother are symbolic, first of all, of the natural urge to establish moral and physical ascendency over a younger member of the family group, and secondly of a manifestation of the unconscious wish to return—if only vicariously—to the element from which we all evolved.'

. . . A human touch was added to the analysis by the psychiatrist's final comment over a cup of tea which

12

was found, after Master Slatterwick had left, to contain the stewed corpses of 27 maggots:

'If that little bastard comes near me again, I'll strangle him, so help me!'

Mr Frederick Hackthorpe, aged 53, Cross Lane, Salford:
'I go fishin' every Satdy an' Sunday wi' the lads. We genly get a coachload up, yer know. We meet round at t' Bale o' Cotton first, like, an' t' landlord lets us in fer one or two while we sort out the crates fer the coach. Nothin' fancy, like. Just a couple o' crates o' Guinness each, an' a crate o' light ale, an' praps 'arf a bottle o' Scotch fer t' bank in case it gets cold.

'We genly start suppin' as soon as t' coach moves off. That stuff doesn't travel well, yer know. Then we arrive at River Weaver an' we 'ave one or two in t' pub just ter get usselves acclimatised, like. Then we get crackin' wi' the fishin', like, burrif it's cold and t' fish aren't tekkin' too clever, like, we leave t' rods on t' rests and go back for a jar or two while things warm up a bit. If there's nowt doin' at all, like, we stay in till closing time in th' afternoon, an' then tek some crates back fer t' journey 'ome.

'If t' driver teks it steady, they're genly open again by the time we get to Salford, so we stop off at social club for the rest o' t' night, like. Sometimes th' wife comes down if there's nowt good on t' telly an' if she's got any money on 'er we mek a real good night of it.

'Ay, I like fishin'. Teks yer out of yerself, like.'

Our Resident Psychiatrist reports:
'Mr Hackthorpe represents a generation of north country working-class men who are used to working hard and playing hard.

'He obviously enjoys the company of his fellow

men, probably finding in their presence an expression both of the unconscious herding instinct and the solidarity necessary to those whose lives are spent as units of mass labour in an urban industrial environment.

'The fact that he welcomes the arrival of his wife at the social club indicates a basic heterosexual outlook and a willingness to accept the family unit, based on monogamy, as an integral part of the social structure.

'The unwillingness to stay by the water in the face of inclement weather conditions points to the fact that he feels slightly ill at ease in the face of the natural elements, and that he regards the actual angling operation as symbolic rather than something from which to gain prolonged enjoyment.

'The consumption rate of alcoholic refreshments before, during and after the fishing points to the fact that Mr Hackthorpe is a drunk.'

Mr Elijah Witherspoon, aged 85, Potbank Crescent, Burslem:
'I still go fishing a bit, but I do more watching nowadays. Fishing isn't what it was, you see. In the old days we used to spend hours digging for worms every morning and when we'd got a couple of sacksful we'd go and tip them in the river. Every morning for six days we'd do that. Then on Sunday morning, with the dawn mist lifting off the fields, all the young lads and girls would climb on to a haycart and we'd ride down to the river.

'Oh, there were some real goings-on, I can tell you. All the lads wore corduroy knee breeches and their best homespun shirts and all the girls wore their long dresses and flowered hats and carried parasols.

'When we got down to the river we would empty another sackful of worms in for luck and the lads

14

would start fishing. We used to catch so many barbel and chub that we needed a farmcart to carry them off. Fish after fish, all beauties—much bigger than anything you see caught today.

'Then when the sun was up and the fish stopped biting, the girls would spread out cloths on the grass and open the picnic baskets. There was chicken and rabbit and veal pies and great sandwiches of crusty bread and bottles of cider. All around, as the sun rose higher, was the scent of the grass and the flowers, the gentle murmuring of the breeze in the trees and the droning of honey bees.

'The gentry would come down in their carriages from the big house and look at the catch and say they had never seen such fish before. Lord Derby himself was a guest at the house once and he said to me: "Witherspoon," he said, "I've never seen anything like it," he said. "Thank you, your lordship," I said, "thank you very much," I said. "Any time you are around Knowsley way," he said, "drop in and see me," he said. "Drop in and see me . . ."

'Oh, and after we'd finished our picnic, what fun we had. We chased those girls all over the fields and all through the woods and rolled them in the buttercups, we did. And then we all went home on the haycart.

'The youngsters these days don't know what they're missing. They don't make their own fun like we had to do. They don't know half . . .'

(At this point Mr Witherspoon nodded off and the interview was discontinued.)

Our Resident Psychiatrist reports:
Mr Witherspoon's retrospective view of angling in his early youth is inevitably enhanced by the distance in time. He sees angling in idyllic terms with a

15

strongly marked emphasis on the conventional picture of rustic life at the turn of the century.

It is known to psychiatry as the Cider-with-Rosie Syndrome.

There are a few reminiscences which do not quite tally with the history of either Mr Witherspoon or the area. Such as the fact that there have been no barbel taken from this particular river since 1847; that it would take ten men a week to dig one sackful of worms; that any girls in summer frocks who travelled on a haycart to the river in the early dawn would catch pneumonia on the three-hour ride; that the owners of the big house employed a gamekeeper with a shotgun specifically to keep anglers off the river; that Lord Derby never came within miles of the place. There is also the fact that Mr Witherspoon was formerly an itinerant actor who never set eyes on this area until twenty years ago, since when he has been kept in cider by telling the same story in every pub along the river.

'Mr Witherspoon is suffering from senile fantasies of a Utopian and Arcadian nature, using them unconsciously as a defence against the harshness of contemporary reality. Mr Witherspoon in short, is a bloody old fake.'

CHAPTER TWO

Tackling Up

An angler spends a great deal of money every year on tackle. The tackle industry itself is really big business. It has been estimated that, with the cost of tackle, bait, clothing, travelling and refreshment, the cost of each fish to the average angler works out at about £14.35.

It is obvious, therefore, that the angler must choose his tackle carefully if he is to get the maximum return for his outlay. In this chapter we deal with the choice, purpose and method of use of the basic tackle and equipment. The angler who reads it carefully, absorbs all the information and applies it to the purchase and use of his gear, should be able within a few weeks to cut down the average cost of each fish to £14.25.

The Rod

Choose a rod which suits *you*, which matches *your* personality and physique. But remember that there are limits to the extent to which personality and physique can be applied to a rod. One angler was ejected recently from a tackle shop after asking for a pot-bellied, shortsighted rod with a raging thirst.

Test the rod in the shop and test it with a reel fitted. Asking the tackle dealer for a reel might seem to be putting him to a lot of trouble, but most of them will reply to the request with a cheery 'Get out!'

Try balancing the rod, just above the reel, on your forefinger. If it snaps in two, it is obviously not as strong as it might be.

Now try a few dummy casts. If, on the first movement, you fall flat on your back, either the rod is too heavy or you ought to eat more Bickiweet for breakfast. If, on the forward movement, the top joint snaps, you can be certain of one thing: you'll have to pay for it.

The Reel

There are three main types of reel: the *centre pin*, the *fixed spool* and the *multiplier*.

The centre pin is the wheel-type reel. It generally has a ratchet mechanism, the main purpose of which is to give early warning of sand in the works.

The fixed spool reel has a stationary bobbin, from which the line is pulled off by the action of the cast, and a line guard. The line guard is the thing around which you always take the line the wrong way when you are making up your rod. You generally find this out when you try to reel in after the first cast.

The multiplier has a system of gears which turns the drum several times for every turn of the handle, thus making for faster recovery. The multiplier is excellent for making birds' nests in the line.

Care of reels is simple. Strip off the line, dismantle the reel, and put all the parts in methylated spirits to soak. When the parts are thoroughly clean, take them to the tackle shop and see if the man can put them back together again.

Hooks

There are three basic hook shapes: *round bend*, *crystal* and *model perfect*.

The round bend has a bend which is round, so that worms don't feel too uncomfortable on it. If there's anything a worm can't stand it's having to hang about,

18

feeling cramped, on a crystal.

The crystal starts as a round bend, then turns sharply upwards. There is doubtless a good reason for this.

The model perfect is a patented design in which the point is offset at an angle. This makes the hooks more certain to penetrate a fish's lip or an angler's earhole.

Split Shot

These are, strangely enough, shot which are split. Their purpose is to give additional weight for casting and for carrying the bait down to the fish.

They should be pinched on to the line with pliers, but most anglers use their teeth. The high incidence of gaps in fishermen's front teeth puts them in great demand for long-distance spitting contests.

The Keepnet

The main purpose of the keepnet is to keep the beer cool, but many anglers use it also for keeping fish alive until the end of the day, when they can be returned unharmed to the water.

It is best to buy a big one, the biggest you can afford. This not only makes sure that the beer gets the maximum flow of cooling water and that the fish are kept healthy and happy; it looks good as well. Other anglers on the bank will look at your outsize keepnet, glowing with admiration of the confidence and skill of a man who expects to fill it, and will be making awestruck comments such as 'Cleverclogs', 'Big 'ead', and 'Cocky sod'.

Though the net be never so big, make sure that the mesh is small. It can be embarrassing to have your catch swimming straight through the holes.

Floats

The average angler has a collection of 673 floats and 4,258 bits of float with which he intends to do something one of these days. Out of the 673 floats he uses two. The rest are for playing with.

Among the traditional games played with floats are:

Soldiers On Parade. The floats are lined up in rows, graded according to size, graded again according to colour, picked up one by one and drooled over, and then put back down again.

See What I've Got. The floats are grouped together in categories and laid out on display. All the bubble floats are put together, all the quill floats, all the balsa floats, all the antenna floats, and so on. A neat label on a piece of white card, bearing the name of the type of float, is laid under each collection. After a drool, the whole lot is bunged back into the tackle box, all mixed up and ready for the next sort out.

The Money I've Spent. Each float is assessed at its retail price and the total added up. The angler works out the final sum in terms of pints of draught bitter. Then he breaks down and cries.

I've Got A Bite. A float is held up, level with the angler's eyes. He jigs it up and down, simulating the movement caused by a biting fish, and makes noises like 'dum-dum-dum'. Then, with a cry of 'BERDOOOOM!' he jerks the float down and under the imaginary surface of the water and yells 'STRIKE!!!!' at the top of his voice. This game is best played in a soundproof room if you don't want to be taken away.

Bobbing In The Bath. This is a great advance on the old-fashioned rubber duck. Before a bath, you prepare several floats by tying a small length of weighted line on the bottom of each. When these are floating around in the bath with you, you can reach under water, tug at a line, and see the float disappear as if a gigantic fish has taken. An advanced version of the game uses hooks on the end of the lines, but this is not recommended to beginners who wish to avoid doing themselves a mischief.

Making Your Own Floats

By making your own floats at home you can save pounds and finish up with floats which look just as good as the shopbought ones, even though they do have a tendency to get waterlogged and sink after the first ten minutes.

There are so many different kinds of float that it would be outside the scope of this volume to attempt any detailed instruction on float making. And it's dead boring, anyway.

Instead, study the illustrations of the revolutionary new Gooligear range of floats. Kits for these, with full instructions, are available for only £35.83p each.

The Gooligear Airborne Float (for flying fish)

21

The Underwater Float (for anglers who don't like float fishing)

The Killer-Diller Fragmentation Float (explodes at the first nibble)

The Lighthouse Float (for night fishing)

The Bardot Float (for making the whole thing more interesting)

The Fishing Basket

There are three basic types of fishing basket: the fly fisher's creel, the coarse fisherman's wicker basket and the steel-framed canvas basket.

The fly fisher's creel is very pretty and is OK for the fly fisher. Apart from that, it's not much use. It won't hold bottles or packets of butties, and you can't sit on it.

The coarse fisherman's wicker basket is sturdy, box-shaped and set on four strong wooden legs. It holds bait, tackle, bottles and butties and you can sit on it, stand on it, jump on it. Some really coarse coarse fishermen have been known to make love on it.

It has the one drawback, however, of causing the condition known to medicine as Basket Bum. Eight hours on the undulating wicker surface transfers a deeply indented reverse image on to the subcutaneous fat of the gluteal muscles. This image can last for 24 hours. While it does no physical harm, it is aesthetically undesirable. Anyone unwilling to wait for the pattern to fade can attempt to remove it by soaking the affected part in hot water and ironing it through a sheet of brown paper. This is, however, a

23

difficult treatment to carry out. If the iron slips it can lead to all sorts of complications.

The steel-framed basket has the advantage of being roomy, light and rigid. The disadvantage is that the frame can cut into the flesh even more deeply than wicker. And anyone who sits down heavily on the sharp edge of the basket can do himself a very nasty nasty.

The Fishing Stool

Folding fishing stools have helped a great deal to cut down the incidence of Basket Bum. Great care has to be taken, however, to ensure that the stool is fully opened before one sits down. A stool of the scissor-type which closes under a descending angler can do a mischief before which the most severe case of Basket Bum pales into insignificance.

The Fishing Umbrella

The big fishing umbrella with the six-foot canopy is useful for keeping off wind and rain, and invaluable for mixed fishing. Behind it you can do things which would otherwise get you locked up.

It has the disadvantage of becoming airborne in a high wind. Slightly-built anglers, grabbing at the shaft of a rising umbrella, have been known to do a Mary Poppins and finish up in the next county.

The Rod Holdall

This is a very useful and dashing piece of equipment. It holds all the rods and bits of tackle and can be carried over the shoulder like an Afghan long rifle or a bazooka.

This resemblance to a firearm lends added

enjoyment to the walk down the river bank. If nobody is looking you can play Davy Crockett, Daniel Boone, John Wayne, the Northwest Frontier, the Alamo or the Battle of the Bulge.

Since the appearance of the holdall on the market, the number of hours spent fishing has gone sharply down, while the number of hours spent playing Cowboys and Indians has gone sharply up.

The Foot Muff

Still regarded by some as a luxury or strictly for the fairies, the foot muff is nevertheless a great source of comfort to the winter fisherman. There is a tendency to forget, however, that *both* feet are in the muff. Many anglers who have jumped up, muffed, to grab the landing net have added significantly to the number who have finished up in the drink.

Waders

These thigh-length rubber boots enable the angler to walk into midstream without getting wet, assuming that both the stream and the angler are of normal proportions.

Short anglers have much more trouble with waders than tall ones. Apart from the discomfort and possible danger of having tough rubber edges sawing away in the most fright-making places, the short angler is much more likely to get that sudden chill round the whatnots[1] which signals 'waders awash'.

When this happens he must not panic, but must turn gently over and float upside down, with his feet sticking out of the water, until he is hooked by an overhanging branch. If there are no overhanging

---

[1] Ankles. What else?

branches, he must try to hold his breath until he passes a lifeboat station.

In common with skindiving suits, plastic macs, PVC trusses and other garments made from smooth, non-porous materials, waders have sexual connotations which are beyond the ken of the average sex maniac such as you or I. The sight of a man in waders has been known to do the strangest things to the most mature of matrons, and has been responsible for many a disastrous ending to a mixed outing.

As for the sight of a *woman* in waders—as Lord Justice Longprong said, when delivering judgment in Regina-*v*-Higginson in 1981:[2]

[2] Cyril Higginson, 52, a self-employed nose-flute tuner, was convicted of leaping about the bank in an unseemly manner in pursuit of Miss Gladys Ewge-Bristoll, of pinching her right buttock and of attempting to fill her waders with black treacle.

'It may well be thought that 93 years' solitary confinement[3] is a sentence of undue severity for this offence, and that the accused was subjected to provocation above and beyond the endurance of the average individual.

'You have heard independent witnesses testify that the appearance of Miss Ewge-Bristoll in citron-yellow waders with transparent panels behind the knees to reveal what we were told were a particularly attractive set of dimples—a statement which I confirmed on examination in my chambers—was enough to send even the most respectable male citizen, as one witness put it, completely off his tiny nut.

'This said, however—and I have taken it fully into account in mitigation of the sentence—this said, we simply cannot have people berserking round our river banks with tins of black treacle in search of unprotected wading females. A female person wearing a pair of waders is entitled to the same protection under the law as a female person not wearing them.

'I intend to make an example of this man and I can only hope that, in so doing, I am nipping in the bud a nationwide outbreak of treacle pouring and bum pinching.'

A healthier manifestation of the erotic appeal of waders is the growing practice of drinking from the waders of the lady of one's choice, much as the stage door Johnnies would drink champagne from the shoe of a Gaiety Girl.

Because of the volume held by even one leg of a pair of waders, drinking champagne is out of the

[3] Mr Higginson's sentence was later commuted on appeal to one of 92 years' solitary confinement.

question. The custom is, instead, to fill the wader with draught bitter or brown and mild. Seasoned drinkers, whose object of adoration is a small woman, have been known to drain one leg in a single breath, notwithstanding the airlock which forms when the level of the ale reaches the knee.

Anglers still mourn, however, Wee Willie Chuckerbutty, whose chosen one was Big Bertha ('All Together Now') Heftipeece, a seventeen-stone former principal boy.

It was revealed at the inquest that Miss Heftipeece's left wader held fourteen gallons of bitter.

Mr Chuckerbutty was unable to raise the full wader to his lips and had to resort to climbing on a table, leaning over, and sucking up the beer through a plastic tube.

He had drunk no more than three gallons when he over-balanced and went in head first. His shoulders became jammed and his friends were unable to extricate him in time.

The coroner noted, as a possible source of consolation to Mr Chuckerbutty's sorrowing family and friends, that at least he died with a smile on his face.

CHAPTER THREE

Freshwater Baits

It used to be rumoured in Manchester that the inhabitants of Salford all suffered from a massive physiological abnormality[1] occasioned by the amount of chips they ate. The rumour is, of course, absolutely without foundation, in spite of the fact that Salfordians do eat chips with everything.

None of this has anything to do with freshwater baits except to illustrate the point that most anglers offer their quarry a diet as unvaried as that of the unfortunate Salfordians. Most anglers will use maggots, bread and worms and nothing else. Some will even fish for a lifetime using only one of these. So this chapter, apart from dealing with the three common baits, will examine some of the other possibilities.

Presentation of Bait

Fish have a keen sense of smell and will reject any bait which is in the slightest bit tainted. Strong smells, such as those of tobacco, onions, socks or *Un Nuit d'Amour*, are especially off-putting.

So before handling the bait, the hands should be thoroughly washed, pumice-stoned and rinsed in running water. To be absolutely sure, the angler should don a gauze mask and rubber gloves before taking the lid off the maggot tin and even then, for

---

[1] A full description of the abnormality belongs to the columns of *The Lancet*, rather than to the pages of this book. I have heard, however, that the same thing can happen to people who are over-fond of pineapple chunks.

preference, use forceps to put the maggot on the hook.

It should be remembered that even the cleanest hands can become tainted, and the serious angler should eschew any form of back-scratching, head-scratching, feet-scratching, belly-scratching, nose-picking or woman-stroking while on the bank. Should any of these habits be indulged in inadvertently, the angler must strip off, scrub down and start all over again.

Apart from tainted bait, fish are also repelled by smelly feet, BO, halitosis, hairy legs, hammer toes, knock knees and fluff in the navel. They also dislike the smell of deodorant.

Maggots

The breeding of maggots is dealt with fully elsewhere. The one thing to remember in their use, when putting the hook in, is to nick it through the skin at the blunt end, just above the 'eyes'. The eyes are not really eyes; maggots don't have any. Eyes at that end wouldn't be any good, anyway, unless the maggot spent its life walking backwards. Scientists are agreed that, whatever the eyes are, it's a funny place to have them.

Maggots can be dyed to make them more attractive to the fish. That's the theory, anyway. The fish don't give a damn.

The maggots can be dyed yellow, blue, violet, brown and pink. The proportion of anglers who use dyed maggots can be worked out by counting the number on any given bank coloured yellow, blue, violet, brown or pink (the anglers, not the maggots).

Worms

Worms, the classical bait for all kinds of fish, are not just worms. There are about fifty species in British

31

soil, and learning to tell the difference is one of the less fascinating of angling pastimes.

They have a very interesting sex life, each worm having a set of male and female reproductive organs. Once the question of who-does-what-and-with-which-and-to-whom has been resolved, the whole thing is presumably quite jolly.

A worm, however, cannot fertilise itself: it needs another worm. This is just as well, otherwise they would not put so much effort into tunnelling all over the garden. They would just lie there, smirking.

The three most common varieties of worm are the *lob worm*, the *red worm* and the *brandling*.

Both red worms and brandlings can be found in manure heaps. The brandlings are smelly, which is why there aren't so many of them. Even their best friends don't fancy them.

The lob worm, the big, fat, juicy garden worm, can be got in quantity by digging over the flowerbeds. This makes it a great favourite with anglers' wives: at least *something* in the garden gets done.

A more exciting way of catching them is to stalk them on the lawn, or in a field, with a torch on a dewy night. As a light footfall is essential, the stalking is best done in stockinged feet.

As soon as the worm is spotted it must be leapt on and grabbed by the tail before it can retreat into its hole. (It keeps its tail tucked into the hole while it sniffs about, and retreats backwards.) Telling the difference between the head and tail under the conditions and at such short notice is difficult. This is the reason why so many half-worms are caught.

Night stalking, for all its fun and excitement, has its drawbacks. The combination of stealth, darkness, dew and stockinged feet leads to a high incidence of pneumonia and arrests.

Worms can be brought to the surface of a lawn by pouring on a strong mixture of salt and water. This completely clears the lawn of worms. And weeds. And grass.

Before the worms are used they must be scoured by putting them in a tin full of florist's moss and turning the tin every twelve hours. This means that by the time they have worked their way to the bottom, they find themselves at the top again. The clever ones cotton on quickly and stay in the middle, whiling away the time with a sexy-looking boy/girl or girl/boy friend.

One variety of worm (called the Blue Head, possibly because its head is blue) can hold its breath longer than the ordinary lob and so can put up a better performance underwater. Which is no doubt some small consolation to it.

Bread

Bread is a very popular and pretty dreary bait. It doesn't wriggle and it doesn't even look all that exciting. It can be used as paste, crust, cube or flake. Paste and crust will stay on the hook long enough to reach the water. Cube and flake generally fall off as the line is cast out.

Wasp Grubs

All you need for a plentiful supply of wasp grubs is a wasps' nest. This may be found in trees, lofts, gaps in masonry, and can be recognised by the presence of several thousand adult wasps, none of whom are likely to take kindly to the abduction of their kiddiwinks.

Shoo the adult wasps away and make off with the nest. When you leave hospital, put the nest in a slow

Shoo the adult wasps away and make off with the nest . . .

oven to bake the grubs. It's not a nice thing to do, but they are so soft in their normal state that they will not stay on the hook. If you do not fancy baking them yourself, call in your friendly neighbourhood sadist.

In any event, do not keep the nest lying around too long without doing anything about it. The little grubs will turn into wasps and you will wish you had never picked up this book.

Crayfish

These are excellent bait for chub and can be caught in a dropnet baited with bits of meat. Or they can be hunted by inserting your hand into holes just under the bank.

You can tell, if the hole is occupied by a crayfish, whether it is on its way in or out. If it's going in, you'll feel its tail. If it's coming out, you'll feel its pincers. If the hole is occupied by a rat, either going in or coming out, you'll feel it.

Hempseed

The hempseed is simmered until the skin splits. It smells so badly that before this happens you are generally thrown out of the kitchen.

The seed is put on the hook by pushing the bend into the split in the skin. The hook is then cast out and the seed falls off.

Silkweed

Silkweed is irresistible to roach, dace and chub. You collect it by drawing the hook through the growths on lock gates. While your silkweed hangs around in the water, ignored, the roach, dace and chub are at the lock gates, knocking hell out of the rest of it.

Bloodworms

These are gnat larvae, found in stagnant water and muddy ditches. They can be collected by drawing a tea strainer through the water or by raking a smooth piece of wood through the mud.

This is a bait for the solitary angler. An hour's poking about at the bottom of a drain ensures his solitariness.

Once enough bloodworms have been collected, the only problem remaining is to get them on the hook. They are as thin as cotton thread and only half an inch long. An extra-mural course in brain surgery is a tremendous advantage.

Greaves

Greaves is waste tallow, so unless you live near an old-fashioned candle maker, you might as well forget this one. You are supposed to boil the greaves and then pick out the best bits for hook bait. If you ever do this, you'll wish you *had* forgotten it.

Wild Baits

Garden creatures such as caterpillars, slugs, grasshoppers, earwigs and spiders make excellent baits. When hooked, they get *very* wild.

Baits from the Pantry

These include cheese, peas, parboiled potatoes, raw meat, pearl barley and macaroni. It's always best to ask the wife first, or you might get home to find you've spent all day throwing your tea at the fish.

Groundbait

Soak some old loaves in water, squeeze them out, mix in bran or chicken meal, and you have a good basic groundbait. You can then add your own secret ingredient: sugar, honey, custard powder, tea leaves, Spanish Fly or LSD.

The real purpose of the groundbait is to ensure that no British fish ever goes in need of a square meal.

CHAPTER FOUR

Blending Into The Background

Angling has never been just a matter of clomping down to the water and flinging in a baited hook. Fish are shy, wary creatures, ready to disappear at the first hint of anything untoward. They can see for quite a distance above the water and, through their lateral lines, can feel from yards away the vibration of a footfall, or a carelessly dropped bottle.

First and last, therefore, the angler must be a hunter. He has to crawl stealthily to the water's edge, to stalk the fish, to hide and to stay hidden.

What a fish can see on the bank is governed by the phenomenon of light known as refraction. When light travels at an angle from one medium into a denser one, and vice versa, it bends at the point of change. This is why a straw appears to bend in a glass of lemonade and why those nice Indian lads in South America who keep appearing on telly because they're about to become extinct, always fire their arrows below the fish.

The effect of refraction on a fish's line of sight is to bend it, so that the fish would see a six-foot man but might miss a four-foot one. So, unless you are four feet tall, it is important to keep low enough, or stay far enough back on the bank, to keep under the fish's line of sight. It is also important to eliminate all reflective surfaces on tackle, clothing or person.

Drab is Fab

So we start by eliminating flash. All your clothing should be dark or drab. If all you have are fluorescent pullovers and tangerine bobbly hats, coat them liberally with mud or rub them down with a cow pat.

Spectacle wearers should cover their lenses with anti-flash liquid. Failing this, the spectacles should be:

(a) rubbed with fine emery paper. (This reduces their optical efficiency a little, but is guaranteed to get rid of the flash.) Or:

(b) coated with a weak solution of liquid manure. (This is preferable to mud because of its greater clinging power.) For do-it-yourself enthusiasts, a good general formula is six dessertspoons of cow plonk to half a pint of lukewarm water. The mixture is stirred well, strained through an old keepnet and applied with a sock or fine camel-hair brush. Before the mixture is dry, mark a cross on the centre of each lens with a matchstick. This is essential if you plan to see anything.

Use the remaining manure to coat the face, hands and—in cases of baldness—the head. Alternatively, rub the head with emery paper to a matt finish.

Teeth should be taken out or painted a dark colour. Those fortunate enough to have naturally green or brown teeth can leave them as they are.

All that is necessary now is for the clothing and headgear to be hung with foliage to break up the outline of the body and to blend in with the background vegetation. Choose foliage which is likely to grow on the bank and which is free from garden pests.

(In his inexperienced youth, Gilhooley[1] once

---

[1] Seamus Nigel McGregor Taliesin Hussein François Adolf Giuseppe Abraham Homer Gilhooley ('I wanted him to feel at home wherever he went, the darlin' boy,' said his mother) appears throughout this book in his various capacities. The brains behind Gooligear, Gooliplan, Goolitique, Gooligame and other companies, he has also acted as guide, counsellor and friend in the author's less cautious moments.

hung himself about with an assortment of plants from his herbaceous border. Not only did the hollyhocks give away his position, resulting in a completely fishless day, but he contracted a severe attack of earwigs and clematis wilt.)

Getting from home to the water in full camouflage gear is not without its hazards. Though the wearing of liquid manure and foliage is not in itself illegal, it has been known to invoke certain statutes and bye-laws such as causing the importation of noxious substances on to public service vehicles and the unlawful giving of palpitations to old ladies.

The Approach to the Water

Here we are faced with the twin problems of sight and vibration. Even a fully camouflaged angler can be recognised if he stands upright against the skyline. And what to the angler might seem a soft footfall can be instantly translated by the fish into the clomp of a size 10 wellie.

So, in approaching the bank, crouch low and keep to long grass or undergrowth. For the last fifty yards, drop flat onto the stomach for a commando crawl. This is familiar to all of us who served our country in NAAFI queues from Aldershot to Kuala Lumpur, but might need some explanation for younger readers or for those who picked their ears with a six-inch nail just before the medical.

Make sure, first of all, that your fishing basket, primus stove, camp stool and beer crate are securely fastened across your back. Now hold the rod cases across the chest, with arms crossed and palms upwards, at the same time cradling the rods on the crooks of the arms.

Drop flat on your stomach, or as flat as your

Even a fully camouflaged angler can be recognised if he stands upright against the skyline . . .

stomach will allow, and use the elbows, knees and sides of the feet as instruments of locomotion. The head and the backside should be kept well down.

Before dropping, it is as well to note the distance and direction of the water. There have been innumerable cases of inexperienced crawlers overshooting the bank and falling base-over-rod-rest into the drink. Several survivors have been expelled from their clubs for polluting the swim, using illegal methods of angling, or screaming for help above the permitted decibel level.

Once at the bank, sit up quietly, unfasten the tackle and remove any unwanted bits of cow pat, barbed wire, brambles, broken bottles or Old Man's Beard which may have been picked up on the way. Further camouflage may now be added until you are indistinguishable from the natural growth of the bank.

Even at this point the hazards are not at an end. Ironically, the better the camouflage, the greater the hazard. Wandering dogs can dampen the spirits;

courting couples can distract the attention or carve initials in the most unlikely places; water voles and fieldmice can be painfully unselective about what they nibble at, and woodpeckers will try anything once.

Gilhooley himself was highly unnerved one autumn when a hedgehog hibernated up his left trouser leg. ('He had no throuble at all gettin' in, but the divvil did he want to come out.')

Much research still has to be done on the receptivity of fish to airborne sounds. Current scientific opinion has it that, as strongly as ground vibrations will travel through water, airborne sound does not penetrate.

Even this seemingly harmless research has its martyr. The angling world still mourns Hieronymous (Quacker) Alder, a distant relation of the famous artist, whose researches into sound transmission were cut tragically short.

As well as being an amateur scientist, Quacker was a skilled angler and renowned bird fancier. His speciality was the study of ducks—whence he got his nickname—but it was combining all of these pursuits that gave him the greatest pleasure.

One day he was sitting by the river bank, in full angling camouflage, making duck calls and observing the reactions of the fish. It was, unfortunately, the duck hunting season. At the third 'quack' somebody shot him.

CHAPTER FIVE

Basic Angling Techniques

Here we are by the river. We know already how to stalk down to the water's edge. Now we have to discover where the fish are likely to be, and how to go after them.

The Kind of Fish

The following table gives you some idea of what depth of water the fish are likely to be in:

Still Water	Running Water	
Rudd	Rudd	
	Chub	
	Dace	
	Trout	Top
	Salmon	
	Bleak	
Roach	Roach	
Perch	Perch	Midwater
Pike	Pike	
Tench	Ruffe	
Bream	Barbel	
Eel	Bream	Bottom
Carp	Eel	
	Gudgeon	

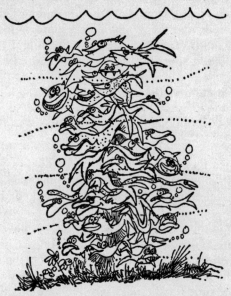

The depth of water the fish are likely to be in . . .

The trouble with tables like this is that the fish never read them. The perch, for instance, is given as a mid-water fish. Which he is, unless he's at the top looking for fry, or at the bottom trying to pick up the odd gudgeon. Tench generally root about the bottom, making a hell of a mess, but when they get fed up of doing that, they'll come up top to see if any crusts have been left lying about. Carp generally wait until the bottom is covered in groundbait and parboiled potatoes before coming up to the bank to suck snails from the lily pads right under the angler's feet.

Where the Fish Are

It is quite simple to work out where the fish are likely to

be. All that has to be considered is the kind of fish, the time of the year, the state of the weather, the temperature of the water, the geography of the river or lake bed, and the availability of natural foods.

You could, of course, simply bait up and cast in a likely-looking spot, but that would be unscientific.

The Weather and the Time of the Year

In hot, summery weather, the fish go off their feed. So you sit there, sweating, without a bite.

In cold, wintry weather, the fish go off their feed. So you sit there, freezing, without a bite.

Most fish can be guaranteed to come back on feed about five minutes after you have packed up to go home.

Careful observation of the weather pays untold dividends. Nip out after a summer shower, when the water will be cooled and oxygenated and the fish will be on the feed again. By the time you have tackled up it will be time for the next shower. You'll get soaked.

In winter, wait for a mild spell and give it three or four days to warm the water before you go out. This will get you to the bank in time for the cold snap and the heaviest snowfall in living memory.

If you fish through a rainstorm, do it under a bridge. All the fish will be there, keeping dry.

The Temperature of the Water

Warm water rises. Cold water sinks. The fish should be at the top, and it's quite a surprise sometimes to find them at the bottom. It's not their fault: by the time they've had a touch of thermocline tilt and temperature inversion, they're not sure where they're supposed to be.

The warm top layer of water in a lake is the

epilimnion. The cold bottom layer is the *hypolimnion*. Between these two is the *thermocline*, neither too warm nor too cold. When wind blows steadily from one side of a lake to the other, the thermocline tilts, building up a layer of deep warm water on the side towards which the wind is blowing. OK so far?

Obviously, the place to catch the fish is on that side of the lake with the wind in your face. This means that almost every time you cast out you finish up with the bait in your face. An angler who has spent several hours fishing the tilted thermocline can be identified easily by his blue complexion, watery eyes, runny nose and the way his ears are turned back to front.

Temperature inversion in a lake happens in winter when the top layer cools and sinks, to be replaced by a warmer layer from underneath. Eventually the whole lake cools to a temperature of 39.2 degrees Fahrenheit, or fourpence three farthings Centigrade, and the water is at its heaviest. At this stage there is no more sinking. The top layer gets colder and colder, but the water at the bottom stays relatively warm.

It is generally still too cold for most fish to feed, but the occasional perch or pike, as daft as the angler sitting freezing on the bank above, may be moving around to see what's about. So you sling in your bait, as deep as you possibly can, to see if you can tempt them. As the perch and pike are surrounded by comatose fish, just waiting to be eaten, you generally can't.

The Volume and Speed of the Water

If you can't locate the river among the flooded fields along the bank, it is safe to assume that there is too much volume. You could, of course, wade out and look for the river, but there is always the risk that you would find it. Your insurance man would not approve.

Speed is generally associated with volume and the river is at its fastest during the winter and spring floods. The speed of the water can be worked out by fixing your eyes on two landmarks and noting the time it takes the uprooted trees, dead cows, overturned boats and floating henhouses to pass between them. Then you can go home.

Natural Food and Underwater Geography

Apart from aquatic plant and animal life already in the water, the fish's supply of natural food consists of animal and vegetable matter, alive and dead, which is blown, washed or dropped into the water. A caterpillar which trips up on an overhanging bush, unless it's a strong swimmer, finds itself as *hors d'œuvres* to a meal of worms, slugs, spiders and flies.

The relationship of this natural food to underwater geography is that it collects in holes, slow eddies behind rocks, and on and around natural snags such as piling, bridge piers, patches of weed, bankside ledges, old prams, sewing machines and bicycle frames.

Thus it follows that where there is food there are fish. And there is also a snag. The trick is to get the fish to take the bait before the bait finds the snag. Statistics show that fishermen are not very good at this.

A plan of the bed of the river is very useful. You can make one by wading across with a Scout's pole and noting the depth every couple of feet or so. If the water goes over the top of the pole, measure the extra depth in handspans. Remember to hold your breath while doing this.

Casting

The purpose of the rod is to get the bait out to the fish. To do this effectively, we have first to learn to cast.

You must learn to cast with a centre pin reel, on the hypothesis that once you can cast with a centre pin you have served your apprenticeship. You can then throw the centre pin away and buy a fixed spool, which makes the whole thing much easier.

Insistence on learning to cast with the centre pin has been perpetuated to a large extent by Seamus Gilhooley. In his capacity as chairman and managing director of Gooligear, he once found himself with three million centre pins on his hands, a purchase he made from a Syrian gentleman who was kind enough to guide his hand on the contract form after a tour of an ouzo distillery in Aleppo.

There are two basic casts in coarse fishing: the overhead and the underhand. The overhead is more popular because it's easier.

To make an overhead cast with a centre pin reel, you grip the rod in the right hand, the thumb against the back of the butt. With the left hand you take the check off the reel and pull off three or four loops of line.

You bring the rod back over the right shoulder and then, with a flick of the wrist, bring it smartly forward, letting go of the loops in your left hand as the line shoots out. Then you put the whole thing down, unravel the loops from your left foot, take the hook out of your ear and try again.

Soon you will get the hang of it and, in so doing, learn a great deal about tree formations and the nesting habits of the commoner British birds.

With a fixed spool reel, everything is laughably

The overhead cast is more popular because it's easier . . .

easy. Curl the right forefinger round the line and hold it to the rod. With the left hand, put the guard in the 'off' position. (This is important: failure to do so will result in your getting an earful of lead and irritated worms.) You use the same motion as for the fixed spool cast, lifting the forefinger from the line as the bait shoots overhead.

The underhand cast is used for fishing from under trees or from a cramped position. With the check or guard off the reel, hold the rod in the right hand and the weight in the left. With a centre pin you have to hold the stripped-off loops of line as well as the weights, which gives the use of the reel another added joy. With a fixed spool the forefinger holds the line against the rod.

Lift the rod and let go the weight. When the weight has swung out to the length of the line, you release the coils or take off the forefinger, depending on the reel.

At the same time you drop the rod tip.

In theory the weight should now soar out over the water to drop in the chosen spot. In practice it drops right at your feet. At this point you move to another pitch where there is room for an overhead cast.

Part of the casting technique involves getting your line down from trees. The classic method is not to wave the rod frantically around until something snaps, but just to pull gently on the line. This does no good either.

You can equip yourself with a range of grappling irons, pruning hooks, ladders and power saws or get philosophical about it and just walk backwards until the line gives way.

Another and vital part of the technique is learning how to get hooks out of earlobes and gluteal muscles, either yours or anyone's who had the misfortune to stand too close.

If the hook has gone in beyond the barb, it is no use trying to pull it back out. You must cut the shank of the hook with a pair of wire cutters and push the point out at the other side of whatever it has gone into.

Surgery on oneself should not be attempted without a generous application of whisky to the inside of the throat. Surgery on someone else can be helped by the use of encouraging phrases such as: 'Close your eyes and think of England,' 'Gad, I can tell you were a commando,' or 'Stop screaming, you damn great poof.'

If the afflicted part is an ear, and the ear isn't yours, you might find it easier all round to cut it off and take out the hook with one swift jerk. Don't throw the ear away: if you call an ambulance quickly enough, they might be able to sew it back on. While you are waiting, don't make jokes like, 'I say, I say, what's this ear?' In situations like that, some people can be hypersensitive.

Striking and Playing the Fish

The float is in the water and the angler is sitting like a crouching cougar, with every nerve, every fibre ready for instant response to the slightest tremor. Or he should be. More likely he is scratching, slumping, dozing, or trying to take off a bottle top with his teeth.

The float trembles. But the experienced angler does not strike immediately. He deduces, from the action of the float, what kind of a fish it is likely to be. A roach, if it does not pull the float sharply under, will nudge it, move it sideways, perhaps lift it. A perch or a gudgeon will give a bob-o-bob before pulling it under. A tench or a bream will fiddle about and lay the float flat before taking it away. A barbel or a chub will take the float straight under with a bang. An eel will fiddle, run, and stop for another fiddle.

As all this goes through the angler's mind, as he attempts to deduce from the actions of the float what kind of monster is at his bait, the fish loses interest and goes away.

The time to strike is when the float dips just under the surface, and the striking movement should be a turn of the wrist—enough to lift the float out of the water and no more.

If more anglers were to remember this there would be fewer reports of unidentified flying objects over canals and fewer stories in local papers about people being struck by gudgeon during freak storms.

Once the fish is on, by design or accident, there is the job of getting him safely to the bank. The first rule is: *Don't Panic*. Nothing is more damaging to the image of the calm, philosophical angler than screams of, 'Omygawd! I've got 'im! I've got 'im!' Especially when the end product is a four-ounce roach with one eye and half a tail.

Rod up, lad. Keep the tip in the air, the line taut and the upper lip stiff. Let the fish do the pulling, give line when you have to, and turn him back with sidestrain. And don't play him for half an hour if all you've got is a three-ounce bleak on a 2½-lb line.

There are two methods of using the landing net: classic and popular.

The classic method is to have the net in the water by the time the fish arrives at the bank. The fish is drawn over the rim and the net lifted up in one smooth, clean movement.

The popular method is to get the fish splashing around at the water's edge and then to give it a karate chop with the rim of the net. The fish leaps, the line breaks. The angler goes running up and down the bank telling everyone what a monster he's just lost, and some poor little fish is left with a mouthful of hook and a thumping headache.

There are classic and popular methods of unhooking fish, too.

The classic method is to take the fish in a wet hand or a damp cloth, ascertain the position of the hook and lift it out cleanly with either fingers or disgorger.

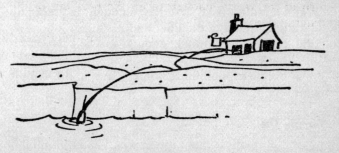

Long trotting

The popular method is to clutch the fish in a hot, dry hand and to wrench out the hook with a fair proportion of fish still attached to it. This leaves the angler wondering why the fish in his keepnet are floating belly-up, and leaves the fish muttering 'Bloody 'ell . . .'

Some Coarse Fishing Techniques

The usual method of float fishing is to fish the swim and hope for the best. There are, however, some variations which may or may not catch more fish, but which at least make your fishing stories a bit less boring. Anyone who can start with, 'There I was, long corking, when all of a sudden . . .' stands a far better chance of keeping his listener awake.

Long Trotting

Long trotting, or long corking, involves sending the float a long way downstream—up to 50 or 60 yards—with the bait just tripping the bottom. The line is paid out from a centre pin reel. Eventually the angler goes cross-eyed from trying to see the float, and when a bite does come he:

(a) Doesn't see it.

(b) Doesn't strike strongly enough to take up the stretch of the line, and misses it.

(c) Does strike strongly enough and falls flat on his back.

An excellent method for dace, chub and Olympic gymnasts.

Laying On

In this method, also known as stret pegging, the line is weighted with several shot, some of which rest on the bottom with the hookbait. The float lies at half-cock, which is a fair description of the way this method often goes off. The theory is that the fish lifts the bait, along with some of the shot. This lifts the float and is the signal for an instant strike. As the fish usually lets go as soon as it feels the weights, and the angler is generally chatting to his mate at the time anyway, the technique has its limitations.

Leger

The line is passed through a drilled weight and a split shot is clipped on, about eighteen inches from the hook, to stop the weight sliding down any further. The fish takes the bait, moves off, and the line slides through the leger weight, making the rod tip twitch.

This can be a useful technique in moving water, or where the bait is wanted on the bottom. The drawback is that, if nothing happens after a while, you tend to fall asleep.

The name comes from the French *leger*, meaning *light*. Most anglers ignore this and use weights the size of a small flat iron.

Float Leger

This is a belt-and-braces technique, using a float attached by the bottom end and a leger weight. Full of false alarms if there is any movement on the water, but at least it keeps you awake.

Sink and Draw

Sink and draw is fishing floatless, with a worm, for perch. The rod is lifted up, then dropped, lifted up, then dropped, as the line is slowly reeled in. If you reel in too fast, the worm gets dizzy. The technique is very popular with yo-yo addicts.

Swingtip

A length of plastic, with a ring at the end, is fixed on to the rod tip. The line is passed through the ring and the swingtip hangs limply down. When a fish takes, the swingtip swings. The angler, who has been watching it swing about in the wind for a couple of hours and has consequently gone into a hypnotic trance, ignores it.

CHAPTER SIX

Some Useful Knots

Knots are very useful for tying things to other things. The full range of anglers' knots can be learned by anybody with an IQ of 140, a Magic Circle Diploma in Prestidigitation and three years to spare.

It is best to practise at home, using an old piece of clothes line. This does you no good at all when you are using invisible nylon in failing light in a snowstorm, but at least you tried. And it does stop you worrying about what you can do with an old piece of clothes line.

Knots have one disadvantage: they are always weaker than the lines they are tied in, so that when you do eventually cast out, the whole of the terminal tackle drops off. But they're fun to do. If you like doing pointless, boring things.

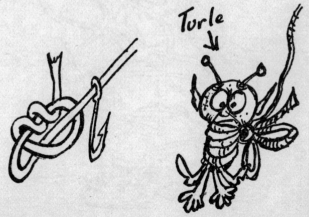

The turle knot   . . . for tying turles

The figure of eight knot

The one-over-the-eight knot

The matchwinner's knot
(to be tied in opponents' lines before the match).

The matchloser's knot

. . . for use when zip breaks

CHAPTER SEVEN

A B To Z Of British Freshwater Fish

Barbel (Barbus barbus)

Lives in fast water in the Hampshire Avon, Dorset Stour, Thames, Severn and in several Yorkshire rivers. Can be recognised by its habit of picking up anything left lying around, big fat mouth and low forehead—characteristics not uncommon east of the Pennines. Has a very sad expression, just like a Tyke who's had to pay for a round. Known to Lancastrians as 'pigfish'. A great smasher of tackle and uneatable with it. For all that, it's lovely. Underneath it all.

Bleak (Alburnus alburnus)

Squitty little silver fish that messes about in shoals on the surface, pecking at floats and snatching at sinking maggots. Often the saviour of matchmen, but with very little else to recommend it.

You can get rid of a shoal of bleak by throwing a crust into the current. As the crust floats downstream, the shoal will follow it. But within thirty seconds another shoal will turn up, then another and another. By the time you have run out of crusts, the first shoal will be back again. Pack up or use a hand grenade.

Bream

The bronze bream (*Abramis brama*) is bronze and the silver bream (*Blicca bjoernka*) is silver.

Remember that.

Both look like an ironed-out roach: very impressive from the side, but from the front they might just as well not be there. Both fight like a wet lettuce.

Carp (Cyprinus carpio)

Carp fishing is a lonely and dedicated art, with a high percentage of suicides and nervous breakdowns among its practitioners. You bait up a spot for days in advance, then sit there all night with a damn great ball of breadpaste or parboiled potato on the hook. Just after dawn the whole thing is chomped up by a shoal of gudgeon.

Chub (Squalius cephalus)

Greedy, bone idle and dead crafty. Loafs about under trees knowing that some idiot is bound to come along sooner or later with a bucketful of groundbait. Likes crayfish, worms, slugs, grasshoppers, breadpaste and Danish Blue cheese. Does not like hooks and spits out anything remotely resembling one.

Anglers interested in fish anatomy can poke a finger down the throat of a big chub and observe the mincing effect of the pharyngeal teeth. For a more objective and less painful observation, ask a friend to do it.

Dace (Leuciscus leuciscus)

Looks like a small chub, but its fins go in where a chub's come out. A handy fish to have around when the temperature drops.

Eel (Anguilla anguilla)

Generally caught when you don't want it, and few people ever do. Catching one means the almost certain irredeemable tangling of terminal tackle and teaches you the aptness of the phrase 'slippery as an eel'. There is nothing, but nothing, slipperier.

Best thing to do is to cut the line close to the hook and let it go. If you want it for the pot, smother it in newspaper, roll it in sand, or drop it into a sack. Clout it hard over the tail and cut its head off. And then go and pull the wings off flies.

Grayling (Thymallus thymallus)

Supposed to smell like thyme. Smells like fish. Beautiful fish, but can't make up its mind whether it's coarse or game. Dray flay men look down on it. Cloth cap lads think it's too good for them. So on the whole it doesn't do too badly.

Gudgeon (Gobio gobio)

Looks like a little barbel with spots. Nice little fella: takes your bait on a hot day when nothing else is moving. Ounce for ounce he fights better than any of them but he will have to put a bit of weight on to make the big time.

Perch (Perca fluviatilis)

Can be recognised by the pain across your palm if you pick him up the wrong way. His spiny dorsal spine does a neat flick-knife job. Can't resist a big fat lobworm.

Grilled with butter, tastes much better than trout. Trouble is, you have to kill him first, and he's much too beautiful for that.

Pike (Esox lucius)

Wicked old sod, all cold eyes and teeth. Looks straight at you as you bring him to the bank and frightens the pants off you. Less wicked than anglers who catch him on livebait and then stomp all over him.

Roach (Rutilus rutilus)

Gentle little darling, found all over the place. Takes anything small to medium you care to offer. Has a tendency to pick up nasty diseases which don't do her any good at all.

Rudd (Scardinius erythrophthalmus)

Looks like a roach after a body building course. Feeds on the surface and likes floating crust. You can catch her after you've clobbered the bleak. Has an anti-social tendency to dive for the weeds when hooked.

Ruffe (Acerina cernua)

Horrible, greedy, spiky, ugly little twit. Apart from that, he doesn't have much to recommend him.

Salmon (Salmo salar)

Noble, big and beautiful. Unfortunately caught up in the British caste system as a status symbol. Is generally much nicer than some of the people who catch him. Has an adventurous career, but his sex life isn't up to much.

Tench (Tinca tinca)

Stands on his head to feed and makes a hell of a mess on the bottom. Fiddles about with bait for ages before he takes. The legendary 'doctor fish', he is supposed not to be eaten by pike. Nobody's told the pike yet.

Trout (Salmo trutta)

Overrated. Thick as two short planks. Trout anglers will argue for hours about which fly he prefers. Meanwhile, he's quite happy with a damn great worm.

Zander (Stizostedion lucioperca)

Known as the pike-perch. Except it's neither pike nor perch, nor any permutation of the two. First imported to Britain from Schleswig-Holstein in 1878. The Great Ouse River Board brought some over in 1960, since when they have bred like rabbits and grown like stink. Very nearly the cause of a civil war once or twice, and guaranteed to cause a punch-up at any anglers' question time.

CHAPTER EIGHT

Some Angling Terms And Their Meanings

A

Absence habits. In scientific usage, the period spent by salmon kelts in the sea before coming back to the rivers.

In domestic usage, the period spent by the angler away from home every weekend.

In angling usage, the period spent by the angler away from his rods in the *Ship and Shovel*.

Alder. A little fly used by trout anglers, a member of the *Sialidae*. It is a brown insect with smooth, veined and sloping wings that fold backwards.

Also the name of a smooth, brown angling artist with a veined and backward-sloping forehead, known on occasions to be a little fly.

. . . known on occasions to be a little fly.

Alewife. Another name for the Allis and Twaite Shads, members of the herring family, also known as Mayfish, Scotch Herring, Twait or Twaite.

Can also indicate a fishing widow who has taken to the bottle.

Ancient wife

Ancient wife. Another name for the Ballan Wrasse, also known as Old Ewe, Sea Swine and Sweet Lips.

An affectionate term used by sea anglers for their spouse, along with Old Moo, Sea Swine and Vinegar Chops.

Angler's curse. A small black fly. Alcoholism. Chronic piles.

Angling. Angling has come to mean the art of fishing with a rod, line and hook, to the exclusion of fishing with spear, net, lasso or hand grenade.

The word comes from the Greek 'Angler', meaning elbow, which was also used to signify anything bent. Elbow bending has ever since been an integral part of the angling ritual and has been held, by some uninformed sources, to have overlaid the original intention of the sport.

Antenna float. Float with a thick, heavy body and long, pointed head (see *Ancient wife*). Used in windy conditions with only the long, thin tip showing. Responsible for 90 per cent of eyestrain among anglers.

Anti-kink device. Depends on the kink. The anti-kink device can be anything from a ball-bearing swivel to a slap on the wrist or a punch up the throat.

August jumpers. Denbighshire name for sea trout. Also the name given during that month to anglers who are careless in the nettle beds.

B

B.S. Breaking strain. Applies either to fishing lines or the tolerance-threshold of an angler who arrives at the pub two minutes after closing time.

B.W.O. Blue Winged Olive. A lovely girl.

Babbing. Fishing for eels with worms threaded on wool. Not to be confused with *babbling*, which is what the angler does when his breaking strain (q.v.) proves unequal to the occasion.

Backlash. What happens when a reel overruns during a cast resulting in a bird's nest of line.

Often the reaction of the angler's wife on his arrival home, late and falling about, from the angling club's social evening.

Bailiff. An officer appointed under the Salmon and Freshwater Fisheries Act of 1923 to enforce the angling bye-laws. Has certain powers of confiscation and arrest without warrant. Usually a reasonable bloke, he will sell you a day ticket if he catches you without one. Then he'll tell you that the stretch you've bought the ticket for doesn't hold any fish. You've got to laugh.

Bait. Anything used on a hook to attract fish. A live bait is generally a fish or frog used to catch pike or perch. Whether the live-baiter gets his kicks from catching the fish or knocking the bait about still has to be determined.

Maggots and worms, for some reason, are not classed as livebaits. They are certainly very active for deadbaits.

Among the more offbeat baits are banana, bacon, macaroni, sausages and bullock's pith. A cry of 'Pith off!' along the river is the traditional warning that an angler has lost his hookbait.

Barbel or barbule. A sensitive feeler, usually on the lower jaw of a shortsighted fish, to help it find food.

The sound made by an angler going down for the third time ('Barbel, barbel, barbel . . .').

Bar spoon. A type of spinner. Used for stirring Bloody Marys.

Bass. The sea perch, *Morone labrax*, from the family *Serranidae*. Gives intoxicating sport.

A beverage retailed by Messrs Bass Charrington. Gives intoxicating sport.

Bastard brill. A small flatfish of uncertain parentage.

Belly. A half circle of line between the rod tip and the float.

The surplus layer of subcutaneous fat which hangs over the angler's belt.

Bite. The taking of bait by a fish.

The taking of bits of angler by gnats, midges, horseflies and stray dogs.

Black spot. Spots on the skin of freshwater fish, notably roach, caused by the larvae of a *trematode*.

Spots on the skin of junior anglers caused by the sparing use of soap and water.

Bottom. The last bit of the terminal tackle, either of the fishing line or of the fisherman.

Brace. Two fish, as in a brace of trout. Or four supports for the trousers, as in a pair of braces.

Bulge. The hump made by a fish taking a bait near the top without breaking the surface. See also *Belly*.

Bung. The large float used in livebaiting for pike.
An obstruction in a barrel to the slaking of a thirst.

Angler's term for 'Would you please be so kind as to pass . . .', as in: 'Bung us the groundbait, mate.'

C

Cabbage patch. Beds of a certain kind of water lily which grow just under the surface of the water. A great boon to the Tackle Manufacturers' Association.

Calvered salmon. A pickled salmon. Not to be confused with a calvered angler.

Casting. The act of presenting bait, lure or fly with rod and line, the object of which with some anglers seems to be the entanglement of the terminal tackle with the nearest tree, hedge, telegraph pole, pumping station, passing tram or old lady.

Chumming. American term meaning to groundbait for sharks. Its use was banned, on the grounds of possible misunderstanding, after a pierhead fracas between a Wigan colliery angling outing and one from the Gay Liberation Front.

Coracle. A light, portable craft, of Celtic origin, consisting of a wicker frame covered with tarpaulin. The angler is supposed to land from the coracle before he plays a fish, but because of the craft's unique capsisability, this seldom happens. Makes for an interesting spectator sport.

Coypu. An aquatic South American rodent which has established itself in East Anglia. Looks like a rat, is as big as a terrier, and has been responsible for mass outbreaks of *delirium tremens* among fishermen.

D

Dapping. Also known as daping, dabbing, dibbling or dibling. Specialised method of taking surface feeding

69

. . . mass outbreaks of delirium tremens (See under Coypu)

fish such as chub. The rod is pushed through a tree or bush overhanging the bank, the angler keeping well out of sight, and the bait lowered on to the surface of the water. Once the chub has taken the bait, the only problem remaining is how to get it out of the tree.

Fly fishermen, if they are so inclined, can dibble their dropper. Whatever turns them on.

Dorsal fin. The back fin of a fish, especially noticeable in the perch by anyone who picks it up the wrong way.

Drag. A fitting on a reel to allow tension to be applied to the line.

The pull of the line on the float or fly in a current.

One of the causes of the trouble on the Wigan colliery shark-fishing outing. (See under *Chumming*.)

Duck. A friendly, semi-domesticated aquatic bird with a habit of poking about in bait tins in search of food. Tastes delicious.

Duffers' fortnight. Two or three weeks in late May/early June when the mayfly are hatching and the trout turn suicidal. Keeps novice fly fishers in stories for years.

E

Electrical fishing. Used by river authorities and angling clubs to catch large numbers of fish for restocking. A generator sends a current of 250 volts through the water between positive and negative electrodes. The stunned fish rise to the surface where they can be netted.

Despite the quick returns, it is not a method to be recommended to the individual angler. Firstly, for him, it's illegal. Secondly, there is a very real danger of a short in your shorts.

Evening rise. The time, after a hot summer's day, when the water cools, the flies return to the river, and the trout feel peckish. An evening rise generally finishes about five minutes before you get down to the river.

In coarse angling, the evening rise occurs among the anglers, just about the time the pubs open.

Evil eel. Scottish name for conger. Anybody who wonders why can try fishing for it in a kilt.

Fallen in. A river is deemed to have fallen in when the level of the water has dropped below normal.

An angler is deemed to have fallen in when the level of the water has risen above his ears.

Father lasher. One of a family of sea bullheads known also as scorpion fish, bull rout, sea toad and short-spined cottus.

Alternatively, the name given to the younger member of an angling family who fixes his hook in the back of the old man's neck.

Fishes royal. Whales, dolphins, porpoises and sturgeons, when captured within the three-mile limit or washed ashore, belong to the Crown. If you find one on the shore, either dead or alive, you should report it to the nearest Receiver of Wrecks. It is not recommended that you wrap it up and post it off to Buckingham Palace. According to ancient right, only the head and tail of the whale belong to the Crown. They'd have to send your bit back.

Fishing the water. Casting a fly or bait into all parts

of the water where fish are likely to be is called 'fishing the water'. What else? Anyone who fishes the trees, the bank or a motorway isn't likely to have much luck. The other term for it is 'chuck and chance it'. Which is a bit more like.

Fish leather. The rough skins of rays, sharks and dogfish are used as emery paper by wood and metal workers. The effectiveness of the abrasive qualities can be testified to by any angler who has caught hold of a spinning dogfish. He is generally known to his pals as 'Lefty'.

Flatfish. True flatfish are those which start life as upright-swimming fish and gradually turn on one side, the eyes meanwhile moving round to the top of the head.

Skates and rays are *not* flatfish. Although they are flat, they are still swimming right way up. Nor is any fish which has been stepped on a true flatfish, no matter how flat it has been flattened.

Flavouring. Almost every angler has his own secret ingredient which he adds to the standard groundbait. Custard, curry powder, HP Sauce, brewer's yeast,

black treacle, brown sugar, cocoa, minced worms, toads' eyes, bats' tonsils and many, many others are added all over the country every Friday and Saturday night. They don't make the slightest difference to the fish, but they keep the angler happy.

Flying fish. A herring-like member of the family *Exocoetidae*, which can travel more than 150 yards out of water on its wing-like fins.

Loosely applied to any small fish caught by an angler on a too-hard strike. Length of flight from the water can be anything from the distance to the nearest tree to the 435-yard record set up by Jim (Lash LaRue) Clegg at Eccles in 1937.

Fly tying. Tying one's own flies is a fascinating hobby and results in a collection of hairy monstrosities which work out far more expensive than buying ready-tied ones. It is also guaranteed to send you boss-eyed within a week.

Fog dust. A very fine cloudbait, used mainly by Sheffield anglers. Its use has fallen off since Sheffield became a smokeless zone and the main ingredient became in short supply.

Foul hook. To foul hook a fish is to hook it anywhere other than the mouth or the parts adjacent. It feels good to the angler, because a foul-hooked fish can pull much harder. It doesn't feel so good to the fish (they don't like it up 'em, you know) and a pike with a treble hook in his backside can turn very nasty when you're trying to get it out.

Free fishing. Free fisheries are those for which the angler pays nothing at all. There are very few of them left: riparian owners and river authorities got wise to this one a long time ago. The most famous free fishery is the Thames below the Town Stone at Staines, presented to the citizens of London by Richard I, on condition they stopped calling him Tricky Dicky.

Some anglers, on waters other than the Thames, do manage to fish for nothing by a combination of good eyesight and a swift 200-yard sprint. The practice of bailiff-dodging is, however, highly reprehensible and no right-thinking angler would indulge in it. Unless he was a hundred per cent sure he could get away with it.

G

Gaff. A large hook on a short handle used for landing large fish. Its use needs some skill. An angler with a gaff sticking through his foot hasn't got it.

Gag. A metal spring for keeping open the mouth of a pike during disgorging.

One of the few means of ensuring a quiet evening during a visit by the wife's mother.

Gaper. Largest member of the clam family. Makes excellent sea bait.

See also wife's mother under *Gag.*

Gentles. Alternative name for maggots. More socially acceptable, as in 'I'm just putting these gentles in the fridge, dear.'

Gill. A fish's means of respiration.

An angler's means of resuscitation and spiritual regeneration.

Glutinous hag. A sea fish of the lamprey family. See also wife's mother under *Gag.*

Gumping. Another name for tickling, along with

One of the few means of ensuring a quiet evening . . . (see
Gag)

groping and *guddling*. Immortalised by Sir Harry
Lauder in the song, *Stop Your Gumping, Groping and
Guddling, Jock*.

H

Hackles. The neck feathers of a chicken used in fly
tying. Also the things which rise on an angler when he
discovers someone trying to chicken out of paying his
round.

Haddy char. A member of the salmon family found
in Scottish waters. Also the inquiry of a Scottish
landlady about your early morning tea, i.e.: 'Haddy
char yet, dearie?'

Hairy Mary. A Scottish salmon fly. Not to be
confused with the hirsute barmaid, Whiskery
Winnie, nor with Aunty Mary who had a canary up
the leg of her drawers.

Half cock. A float which is leaning over, away from the vertical, at an angle of about thirty degrees, is said to be at half cock.

An angler who is leaning over, away from the vertical, at an angle of about thirty degrees, is said to be half cut.

Hand lining. A method used when a hooked fish has gone to weed. The angler puts down the rod and pulls gently on the line. Or he tries to annoy the fish with sharp tugs to make it move out. Either way, the line breaks.

Hempseed. A deadly bait, banned on many waters because of its supposedly drugging qualities. No use chewing it or trying to smoke it. It won't turn you on unless you're a canary.

Hips and haws. Use only when ripe. See also *Holding places.*

Holding places. Places where a salmon or trout may lie. Also places where one may get a grip on the barmaid. See also *Hairy Mary* and *Hips and haws.*

Home instinct. The facility of salmon and sea trout of returning to the river in which they were hatched. Also the facility of the fisherman to finish up on his own doorstep, at three in the morning, no matter how many diversions he has met with on the way.

I

Irish shine. Another name for the River Blackwater, Eire. Also the surface glow imparted to the angler's nose after a session on Power's, Jameson's, Bushmill's or Gilhooley's Morning Dew.

Itchen trout. There's only one thing you can do for an Itchen trout. Scratch it.

No matter how many diversions . . . (*see* Home Instinct)

J

Japanese Chin. The smell of Japanese Chin is said to attract sea trout, Japanese Chin is therefore used to scent worms. It is not to be confused with Chinese Nostril, which is something completely different and not to be sniffed at.

Jigging. A fish shaking its head from side to side to get rid of a hook is said to be jigging about. An angler shaking his head from side to side when it's his turn to pay is said to be frigging about.

K

Keepnet. Long net, of circular and/or rectangular sections used by coarse fishermen to keep the beer cool and on occasions to keep the catch in. The size of the net and the number and size of fish kept in it usually work out in inverse proportions.

Killick Stones. Killick Stones, or Sling Stones, are large stones which are lashed to a rope as a makeshift anchor. Another version is a sackful of stones towed behind the boat. Known as Idiot's Anchor, it is recommended for use only by strong swimmers.

Kip. The hook at the end of the lower jaw of the male salmon during its time in fresh water. Its significance is entirely sexual, and it disappears after mating.

Also the state of temporary unconsciousness voluntarily undertaken by a fisherman when nothing much is happening to his float. It has no sexual significance whatsoever, although the urge to kip is sometimes strongly felt after mating.

Knots. These are dealt with elsewhere in the book. It might, however, be worth mentioning the traditional angler's phrase, 'Get knotted', which originally meant, 'May you and good fortune be bound to one another by cords of steel, and may your flies never be untied except in a worthy cause.'

It has since been debased by over-use and has come to mean something rather revolting.

L

Lady of the stream. Another name for the grayling. Nothing to do with the large blonde lady who used to wander up and down the banks of the Trent in search of tired fishermen.

Larger Spotted Dogfish. A large spotted dogfish which is larger than the Lesser Spotted Dogfish (q.v.).

Lash. Also known as stinting. The old name for

gut. points on which flies were tied. Hence the old saying, 'Stint the lash and spoil the fly.'

Lateral line. The row of perforations down each side of a fish, linked by canals to special sensory nerves, through which it feels vibrations in the water. Vestigial lateral lines are found in higher animals, including humans, and can be traced by prodding with the sharp end of a rod rest.

Lay by. A slack part of the river. Also a parking spot by the roadside used by anglers who didn't drive all that way just for the fishing.

Legering. Comes from the French *leger*, meaning *light*. A method of fishing which uses damn great heavy weights.

Length of fish. The length measured from the tip of the nose to the fork of the tail. Multiplied by three when telling the story.

Lesser Spotted Dogfish. A small spotted dogfish which is smaller than the Larger Spotted Dogfish (q.v.).

Lie. The place where a fish waits for food to be brought down by the current. Also known as a *lair* or *hold*. Alternatively, the apocryphal or subjective truth told by one angler to another about the one that got away. Also known as a fib, a whopper, a terminological inexactitude.

Little pig. A round sea fish, also known as sunfish and molebut. Alternatively, the young delinquent who throws stones at one's float from the opposite bank.

Long trotting. A method of swimming the bait a long way downstream where the angler can, with a clear conscience, lose all interest in the float.

The swift run to the pub when the angler has been

For use only by strong swimmers . . . (See Killick Stones)

unwise enough to fish too far away and careless enough not to keep an eye on the time.

Lonsdale's char. The lady who does for Mr Lonsdale.

Anglers who didn't drive all that way just for the fishing . . .
(*See* Lay by)

M

Maiden fish. A female fish for whom Mr Right hasn't yet come along. The causes, apart from extreme youth, can be BO, bad breath, spots, shyness, a possesive mother or a traumatic experience with a lamprey in early childhood.

Mended kelts. Spawned salmon after a re-tread.

Mona's scale. Mona was the name of a contributor to the *Fishing Gazette*. It wasn't his real one, because he was a bloke. In 1918 he worked out a length-to-weight ratio for pike which proved to be remarkably accurate. It is therefore best ignored if you want to get the most mileage out of your monster pike stories.

Music, piscatorial. Angling has its own music. There is, of course, Schubert's *Trout Quintet.* There is also a quintet in D, *The Compleat Angler,* by William

For whom Mr Right hasn't yet come along . . . (See Maiden Fish)

Walton. Better known works, perhaps, are Seamus Gilhooley's *Fly Way, How Much Is That Dogfish In The Window? Gentles On My Mind, Autumn Greaves, Eel Meet Again* and *Tiddler On The Roof.*

N

Narrow entry. A cast made with a tight bow into the wind, to reduce wind resistance on the line. Also used to describe the back way into a pub. Difficult to negotiate when loaded up with gear.

Neck. A narrow strait in a river between high banks, or the end of a pool where the water flows in. The part of the angler covered in brass.

Night fishing. Fishing during the hours of darkness,

a method which accounts for some fish and thousands of anglers.

The best branch of the sport for anyone who doesn't really intend going fishing.

Night Hooks. Hooks pegged on lengths of line and left out overnight for the tide to cover. Not to be confused with Night Hawks, which have a much higher disappearance rate.

Nymph. The larval stage of an aquatic fly. Trout go roving in search of it. Also mythological maidens who swim around starkers, making sure that the fish are happy. Anglers go roving in search of them.

O

Otter. A beautiful aquatic mammal which keeps down the number of eels but which is blasted on sight by keepers because of its liking for salmon and trout. It kept the mounted otter hunts in kicks until hunting and pollution put it in line for extinction.

Also the name of a piece of equipment, made from a piece of wood and length of line, which is sent down the reel line to release tackle caught in weeds or on the bottom. If the otter gets stuck, the angler can make an otter-releasing otter and send that down as well.

Overhead cast. The cast that gets stuck in the trees behind you.

P

Pain in angling. Fish do not feel pain to anywhere near the same degree as more highly-developed, warm-blooded animals. But that's not to say they like it.

Anglers have a much lower pain threshold, as is demonstrated every time one gets a hook stuck in his earhole or impales himself on the dorsal fin of a perch. You don't see fish running up and down the bank yelling blue murder and screaming for an ambulance.

Pharyngeal teeth. These are teeth in the throat of a fish, used for crushing food, and can be located by poking the forefinger into the gullet. For anyone daft enough to want to try it, they are particularly effective in the case of the chub.

Pill. Pollack shoals sometimes encircle a shoal of small fish and drive them inwards. The habit is known as the pill, or pillion. This habit is celebrated in the old song:

> *When the pollack were on the pillion*
> *We used to catch 'em by the million.*
> *But when the pollack were on the bottom,*
> *Most o' the time we just forgot 'em.*

Playing a fish. Keeping contact with a fish once it has taken the bait, and getting it safely to the bank. The golden rules are: exert pressure all the time, even when you are allowing the fish to run; turn its head with sidestrain at the end of each run;

when the fish is at the bank, draw it over the landing net and lift it out in one clean movement.

If anglers followed these rules there'd be a hell of a slump in the tackle trade.

Pleasure angler. The name given by match anglers to those who prefer to fish alone, just for the fun of it. This has corrected those of us who thought that pleasure was what it was all about.

Plug. Artificial baits for predatory fish. Most of them are highly coloured and shaped like small fish. Some are single-bodied, others are jointed. There are some that sink, some that float, some that wiggle and some that pop. Great things to play with. You can even try fishing with them.

Pollution. One of the greatest menaces to our fisheries. Apart from the normal causes—detergent, cyanide, sewage, factory waste and insecticides— there are instances of pollution from anglers' feet and occasionally the whole angler.

Priest. A weighted club for killing fish. One design is called His Reverence. For giving the last rites, you see. Ho, ho, ho. Sick, sick, sick.

Purist. Someone who will use only artificial flies— sometimes only dry flies—and who scorns anyone who uses bait. A right twit.

Q

Quill. Quills from birds' primary feathers are stripped and used to make floats. Crow is the smallest, goose and swan the biggest. Free quills can be had by whipping them smartly out of a goose's parson's nose. This is not to be recommended, however, with the porcupine.

Queenie pool. A **famous** salmon lie on the West Dart. Above the bank is the Pixie Cave, when offerings are traditionally left for the Little People by anyone who wishes to catch a Dart salmon. This has led to the establishment of the nationwide Gilhooley Leprechaun's Lairs, where anyone leaving a £5 note is thrice blessed: twice by Gilhooley and once by his bank manager.

R

Refraction. The principle of light which means that a fish can see a six-foot angler more easily than a four-foot one. Which explains why Toulouse Lautrec swept the board in the Seine Finals of 1886.

Ripe fish. A fish ready to spawn. Not to be confused with the Ripe Fisherman, which is one who has neglected to change his socks.

Rock salmon. Chip-lovers will be saddened to learn that there is no such fish. It's catfish, mainly, followed closely by the lesser spotted dogfish, coalfish and angler fish. Yuck.

Roe. The eggs or sperm of fish. Hard roes are eggs, soft roes are sperm. Some fish have both, which worries them.

Rolling pollack. Another name for a pollack, particularly one which has just been dropped.

Rubby dubby. A string bag full of chopped-up fish heads and guts, hung over the side of the boat to attract sharks. This is the American 'chumming' (q.v.). The man in charge of the rubby dubby doesn't get much chumming. In fact people tend to keep well to windward.

Runt. Old or stunted fish. Old or stunted fisherman.

Ryepecks. The poles driven into the bed of the river on to which you cling when the punt moves away from under your feet.

S

Salmon smoking. Not likely to appeal to anyone used to proprietary brands of tobacco.

Scratching. A local name for greaves along the Trent. A habit of the Itchen trout (q.v.).

Set. A permanent bend in a rod caused by incorrect storage or over-use.

A set in an angler's right elbow, also caused by over-use, is referred to as Boozer's Lock.

Sex of fish. Not always easy to tell, and not very thrilling when you have found out.

Sheffield ducker. A slim float used for Sheffield style fishing. Also a Yorkshireman who has made an incautious remark during an away match in Lancashire.

Shiner. A young mackerel. Also a blemish on the face of an angler, generally in the vicinity of the right eye, contracted either during a discussion on the peg draw or after arriving home late, kissing the cat and putting his wife out.

Shooting a line. Pulling off extra line, holding it in the left hand, then releasing it on the forward cast to give extra distance.

In its conversational context, shooting a line means giving your fellow anglers an objective and unbiased report on the size and number of your day's catch.

Shot grayling. In Herefordshire, a grayling too young to have spawned. Elsewhere, a two-year-old grayling *after* it has spawned, providing the local term

After the preliminary application of a clog iron . . . (See Skull dragging)

isn't *shute* or *shut*. There must be an easier way.

Sipping Rise. The rise of a fish to take a fly from the surface, making little disturbance. Also the elevation on his toes of an angler taking the first pint of the day.

Six gilled shark. A shark, surprisingly enough, with six gills. A six gilled sharkfisher is a three-pint man.

Skull dragging. In the fens, the trailing of a line from a boat. In Wigan, the trailing of an opponent by the hair after the preliminary application of a clog iron.

Spanish fly. Another name for the Needle Fly. Also an aphrodisiac used by anglers with varying effect on continental fishing trips.

Star drag. A tension device for sea multiplying reels.
Danny La Rue's costumes.

Steeple cast. A cast which sends the line straight up behind the fisherman. Designed to avoid trees. If too energetically done, can live up to its name.

Strike. The tightening of the line by the raising of the rod tip to set the hook in the fish's mouth.
One of the forms of industrial action used now and again to allow more time for fishing.

Stripper. The man at the fish hatchery who strips the fish of eggs or milt.

The young lady booked to entertain the angling club after a match.

Sucker. A fat, round, ugly sea fish with a red belly, so called because it can attach itself to stones by means of a sucker. Also the term for a matchman, possibly fat, round and ugly, with or without a red belly, who backs himself for a tenner when Kevin Ashurst is fishing three pegs away.

Sulking. A sulking fish is one which goes to the bottom after being hooked and refuses to budge. Can be persuaded to move by throwing stones in the water behind him.

A sulking angler is one who refuses to leave the bar to watch the presentation of the prizes, none of which he has won. Can be persuaded to move by the promise of a double scotch after the ceremony.

Swim. The stretch of water fished by an angler. Also what boat anglers are obliged to do after stepping back to admire their catch.

T

Tailing. Method of landing a big fish, without the use of gaff or net, by grabbing it round the 'wrist' of the tail. Done incorrectly, it will mean that the fish will slap you in the face and leap back into the water. Done correctly, it will mean that the fish will slap you in the face and leap back into the water.

Ten hundred herrings. Is 1,320 herrings, because a hundred herrings is 132. Or, if you prefer it, 33 warps.

Tickling. Method of catching a fish using only one

hand. Also a sure means of getting your face slapped, whether you're using one hand or two.

Trolling. Either fishing sink and draw with dead-bait, for pike and perch, or walking up and down the bank, impeccably groomed and dishily dressed. Best not to tell your friends you are going trolling if you don't want a reply of 'Oops, dearie'.

U

UDN. Ulcerative Dermal Necrosis. A very nasty disease, but you've got to be a fish to get it.

Umbar or Umber. Old name for grayling. It was the custom in the Middle Ages to put the first grayling caught under one's *jumbar*, or leather jerkin, hence the old rhyme:

> *Umbar, Umbar,*
> *Stick it up your jumbar.*

V

Vera. The lovely barmaid who said I'd be on for a free pint if I gave her a mention. Besides which, there isn't anything else interesting under *V*.

W

Waders. Rubber thigh boots. Short anglers who buy long ones become aware of the strangest sensations under the armpits.

Wading. A guaranteed method of coming home soggy.

Walton, Izaak. An amiable old windbag. Lived from 1593 to 1683 and wrote *The Compleat Angler*

. . . stick it up your jumbar. (*See* Umbar).

in 1653. The charm of *The Compleat Angler* lies in the fact that nobody ever reads it. A very similar book by another, earlier author, has been discovered, which seems to indicate that the old lad cribbed a lot of his stuff—an example which has been followed by angling writers ever since.

Wand. Scottish name for fishing rod. Popular with fairies (see *Chumming* and *Trolling*).

Whipping the water. Casting a fly on to the surface of the water. Not to be confused with Flogging the Flume or Furgling the Foam.

Wreck of the sea. Old term for whales and sturgeons washed up or caught within the three-mile limit. Also an angler back from a North Sea trip in a Force Eight gale.

X

Xanthochroism. The ability of certain fish to alter their natural colouring to gold. Also the only entry I could find under *X*.

Y

Yarrell's blenny. A northern blenny, not to be confused with Montagu's Blenny, the Butterfly Blenny or the Tompot. Nor, for that matter, with Bloch's Topknot or Jago's Goldsinny. How the hell did I get into this?

Z

Zander. You will have read about the zander in Chapter Seven. It's only listed here because there's no other entry under *Z*. I don't even know a barmaid called Zena. Pity about that.

CHAPTER NINE

The Gentle Art

What can be more satisfying or enjoyable than the rearing of maggots at home?

How about that for a bloody silly question? Having got rid of it, we can get down to the nitty gritty. Or, as we say in the trade, the squirmy wirmy.

Maggot breeding has a special appeal for anyone who has a yen for the solitary life. (After a little while the neighbours move away. Followed, shortly after, by the wife and kids.)

Materials are few and equipment is simple. First you need a corpse, preferably in an advanced state of decomposition, the choice of which can be determined by the number of maggots you intend to produce.

You could use, depending on quantity, taste and availability, a horse, a sheep, a cat, a politician or the mother-in-law. The choice of the last, apart from removing one of life's major drawbacks, has the added appeal of keeping the whole thing in the family.

Esprit de Corpse

Acquisition of the corpse is the first step. Betting men can make their choice of horse from the sure thing they were given for the 2.30, the dead cert for the three o'clock, or the arthritic heap of catsmeat they put their shirts on for the last race.

You can pick up a sheep for the price of a fast spin,

at midnight and without lights, over a moorland road.

Choose your politician carefully. Do not be deceived by appearances: comb through the front benches until you find one that really *is* dead. Given a choice, go for one called Ernest. There's nothing flies like better than making love in Dead Ernest.

Mothers-in-law are notoriously difficult to bring to the happy state of *rigor mortis*, most having such an accumulation of bone between the eyes as to render a humane killer ineffective. Recommended methods include:

(*a*) Having her back you in as you park the family steamroller;

(*b*) Taking her:
   (i) to a weedkiller tasting, or
   (ii) for a study of the cliffside flora at Beachy Head.

Most cats have no difficulty in responding to a two-pound hammer.

The dear departed should be hung, out of doors, over a tubful of bran. The site must be carefully chosen: a combination of a southern aspect and the leeward side of the house is ideal. Planning permission might have to be obtained for the horse; an X Certificate for the mother-in-law.

Some are more Equal

All maggots are not equal. This is important to know from the start, if you are not going to breed an inferior product.

There are four main kinds. The little *squats* are the offspring of the common housefly; *specials* come from a bigger kind of housefly; big *liver maggots* come from the bluebottle, and *pinkies* from the greenbottle.

Why a greenbottle should have pinkies is one of the more boring mysteries of modern science.

To avoid having the breeding ground over-populated by squats to the disadvantage of the bigger maggots, some form of selective birth control has to be applied.

Years of research has shown that simply standing there and saying, 'Shoo!' has little or no effect. (This has led many eminent scientists to conclude that houseflies are stone deaf.) Nor can the squirting with insecticide of houseflies in labour be recommended: the overkill is such that many breeding bottles cop for it as well.

The overkill disadvantage applies also to the spraying of flies on the wing with instant aerosol starch. Besides which, the noise of the stiff little bodies screaming down out of control and crashing on to the patio can be quite upsetting to anyone with a sensitive nature.

Subject Normal

Sex is another problem. For every female bluebottle, looking for somewhere to drop one of her 20 batches of 130 eggs, there is a male bottle whose only interest is in a free meal. As a corpse conservation measure, every male bottle should be dealt a swift clout before he can get his teeth into the meat.

Sexing bluebottles with any degree of accuracy, however, is very difficult. Their size makes a close examination absolutely essential and it is practically impossible to get them to stay still long enough for that. More than one breeder, unwise enough to attempt this selective culling, has been carried away suffering from severe eyestrain and the gibbering heebies.

Within two or three days the corpse should be

pullulating with infant gentles, happily slurping their way through the golden, innocent days of childhood. By listening closely, having first taken your nose between forefinger and thumb, it is possible actually to hear the little chaps wriggling and chomping in an ecstasy of exploration and discovery.

After a week or ten days they are fully grown and ready to face the perils of the outside world. They drop off into the tub of bran, and from here they can be transferred into airholed cans for storage.

The Nighthawk Syndrome

While in the can they will need further feeding. Otherwise they may eat each other and even, in moments of mental aberration, themselves.

Research by Mr Seamus Gilhooley into this phenomenon has shown that, given a sufficient degree of flexibility and room for a 360-degree curve, a maggot can disappear altogether without any outside help.

The phenomenon, known to science as the Nighthawk Syndrome, is occasioned by the fact that maggots are:

(*a*) Shortsighted
(*b*) Absent minded
(*c*) Insensitive, and
(*d*) Bloody greedy

Prevention of the syndrome is obviously of the greatest importance, and a great deal of Mr Gilhooley's researches were directed towards this end. He finally perfected a dietetic formula the ingredients of which are:

1 lb butter
1 lb honey
1 oz chilli powder
1 bottle Irish whiskey

Shortsighted, absent-minded, insensitive and bloody greedy . . .

The butter is melted and beaten in well with the honey and the chilli powder. The resulting mixture is allowed to cool. It is then fed to the maggots at the rate of one teaspoonful per tin of 500 maggots per hour.

The effect is magical. The butter imparts a velvet-smooth skin, a rounded profile and a seductive golden glow.

The honey ensures an adequate supply of vitamins and makes the little fellows look younger, live longer.

The chilli powder doesn't half make them jump.

The whiskey, as you may have noticed, was not added to the mixture fed to the maggots. It has a significant effect on their welfare, however, as part of the Tir Na nOg Noshing Ceilidh, a Gaelic ritual akin to the Japanese Tea Ceremony.

The ceremony was discovered by Mr Gilhooley during his researches into the relationship between angling and the fertility rites of Ballyhooly, Co. Cork (the land of his fathers, whoever they were). It ensures happy, healthy maggots, incredibly success-ful fishing, and the full spiritual preparation of the angler.

First, a generous measure of the *uisge beatha* is poured into a tumbler. The tumbler is lifted towards the breeder's nose. After three deep inhalations through each nostril, the following charm is intoned:

> *May St Patrick, St Bride, St Jude*
> *and the four-eyed Chinese saint of*
> *O'Connell Street bless dese little*
> *fellas in dis tin an' give 'em de*
> *sthrength ter sthrangle any fish*
> *dat comes within leppin' distance*

(The Irish accent, while not absolutely essen-tial, adds immeasurably to the effectiveness of the charm.)

Some of the butter and honey mixture is then lifted on a silver spoon. (I noticed that Gilhooley used one inscribed with the Gaelic rune *Bri Ti Shra Il.*) The spoon is then tapped smartly on the rim of the tin to deliver the elixir to the maggots.

In the deeply moving climax of the ritual, the whiskey is drained in three short gulps and the lid of the maggot tin is replaced.

The ceremony should be repeated at every hourly feed. Mr Gilhooley, unfortunately, was not able to specify how many times it could be safely carried out. After the fourteenth consecutive blessing he went into what appeared to be a form of religious trance and slid under the table.

Storage of Maggots

In warm weather, maggots tend to chrysalise very quickly and it is advisable to keep them under refrigerated conditions. This has been known to give rise to domestic friction in cases where the female spouse was not wholly in sympathy with the piscatorial ethos. In such cases a little subterfuge is called for.

The simplest method is to label the tin with the name of some innocuous product before placing it in the salad drawer of the refrigerator. *Bread Paste* or *Cheese Paste* are quite safe: the little woman knows they are something to do with fishing but are also quite hygienic.

Do not on any account use the name of anything which could conceivably be served up in a meal— especially *Long Grain Rice*. This excellent product bears a strong resemblance to maggots in a refrigerated torpor. More than once it has happened that a shortsighted housewife has picked up a tin so labelled and made a curried rice dish for the local babysitting circle. There's nothing *wrong* with it, mind you, but few things are more heartrending for the angler than to find that the maggots he went to so much trouble and expense to breed have been wolfed at one go by a bunch of twittering women.

So long as nobody tells them about it, surplus gentles can be served with safety at meetings of the Weight Watcher's Club. They have an extremely high protein content, are low on carbohydrates and, served curried and with the appropriate sauce, do not taste bad at all.

Coming in from the Cold

In warm weather, the problem is to keep the maggots cold enough to prevent them from chrysalising. In cold weather the problem is to keep them from dozing off altogether.

Old match anglers often keep the maggots under their tongues to keep them lively during the competition, but this is impracticable for bulk or long term storage.

The simplest method of all is to take the tin to bed, but this too has its drawbacks. Apart from inhibiting the sex life of the angler, the presence of the tin makes sleeping rather difficult. There is the added danger of the lid coming adrift in the middle of the night. With half an hour's start, the little devils are very difficult to catch.

The Wisdom of the Dangli Sutra

An ancient Indian method, designed for Ganges match fishing and expounded at length in the *Dangli Sutra* by the piscatorial guru, Chukkitan Chansit, was to keep the maggots under the armpit of a maiden.

These days it is difficult to find:

(*a*) A maiden, or
(*b*) One whose armpit has not been rendered untenable by the use of depilatories and deodorants.

The sad fact is that under an armpit which is hairless, dry and odourless, the little blokes do not feel a bit at home.

Mr Gilhooley carried out an experiment with his own armpit, but the results were hardly encouraging. Out of a total of 100 maggots which were kept under his left arm for eight hours under laboratory conditions.

73 died from natural causes (mainly asphyxia)

 5 suffered severe mental derangement

 9 turned green

13 disappeared (six turning up three weeks later when he changed his socks)

In analysing possible causes of failure, Mr Gilhooley conceded that his maidenhood may not have been all that it should. He put the main cause, however, down to excessive personal hygiene: he had taken a bath a month earlier and his armpit was probably still in a state of carbolicised sterility.

CHAPTER TEN

A Family Affair

Fishing has always been regarded as a solitary sport, the pastime for the contemplative man. It was unthinkable—as in pig sticking, dominoes, pontoon and three-card brag—that women should come within a mile of it.

Of recent years, however, thanks to the increase in leisure time, the number of household labour-saving devices and family cars, the tendency has grown for whole households to go fishing together.

This development has wrought subtle changes in the ethos of the sport. The old image of the angler was that of a loner, a solitary—a misanthrope, even— who went fishing simply to get away from the wife and family. That image gained currency, and survived so long, for one reason and one reason only. It was true.

The influence of the family on angling is demonstrated by the following television documentary which, when it made its appearance, was greeted with a tremendous outburst of public indifference.

The documentary traces the course of a family angling weekend. The wifely monologue is based on actual comments by angling wives whose husbands still have the scars to show for it.

The Changing Face of Angling

The solitary angler was used to falling out of bed in the early hours of Sunday morning, pulling on his familiar and ripe-smelling gear, having a quick scratch and a stiff scotch, and stomping out bleary and blissful into the dawn.

But now that the feminine influence has exerted itself, things are different.

All Saturday morning is spent polishing the car.

If you think you're taking us out with the car in that state, you've got another think coming. Why we can't have a decent car I don't know. That one over the road's been swanking all week about their new one. Only an Aston Martin, that's all. Mind you, there's something funny going on there. I said to Mrs Bates, I said, 'He's not come by that through honest toil,' I said. And when you see her, as well, prancing up and down the road in her fur coat. Mind you, I've never thought much of her. I was only saying to Mrs Bates, I said, 'Fur coat and no drawers, that one,' I said . . .

Saturday afternoon is spent trying on the new fishing outfit. The old outfit is got rid of. The comfortable holey vests, pullover, long johns, saggy jacket, scale-smeared anorak, droopy wellies and bobbly hat are lowered on fire tongs into the dustbin. In their place go an electric blue windcheater with red and white facings, a pair of slimline, knife-edged cream casual trousers, a pair of Italian hand-made slip-on shoes and a tartan trilby decorated with unusable flies.

There, you look ever so smart. I got these from that new anglers' boutique, The Bulging Creel. *The young chap there was ever so nice. He was wearing a beautiful mauve see-through shirt with ruffles all down the front and lots of lace around the wrists. He said that absolutely everyone was wearing them on the canal these days, but I thought it wouldn't last five minutes on you, the way you keep dribbling soup and dropping ash all down you.*

Saturday evening is spent helping with the food.

I've got two dozen fairy cakes, a dozen eclairs, half a dozen maids of honour and a box of Before Nines. Now if you butter the bread, I'll slice the cucumbers and make the curried egg paste. Then I can shell the scampi and stuff the olives. All we've got to do after that is to cream the mushrooms, shred the carrots, dice the beetroot, boil the lobster, chill the avocado, southern-fry the chicken . . . what? No, you can't have cheese and onion butties. You know they give you heartburn, and you're not climbing into bed with me smelling like a garlic warehouse . . .

Early Sunday morning is spent packing the car.

You can take that crate of Guinness out of the boot for a start. That's all you ever think about. Now, check these off to make sure we've got everything. Those twelve plastic boxes have got the cakes and sandwiches; the towels and toilet bags are in the grip. Deckchairs and travelling rugs . . . yes. Primus stove, kettle, frying pan, pound of bacon, dozen eggs, fly spray, sun lotion, wind lotion, hand cream, mother's hot water bottle, mother's Thermogene and Vick, mother's . . .

Of course I told you mother was coming. We can't leave her on her own at her age. She'll be no trouble, will you, mother? No, 'course you won't. She'll just sit quietly and—don't you call my mother that! You've got room to talk with your family. My mother doesn't come home plastered every night like someone's father I could mention. And she doesn't carry on with the gasman like someone's auntie I know. You just keep quiet and make sure those kids have been to the toilet before we go. Oh, our Peregrine, if you're sick all over the car again, you won't half cop it.

All we need now are Bingo's biscuits and water bowl. Of course we're taking Bingo. We can't leave her all alone in the house. Somebody might break in. She'd die if anybody did that, wouldn't you, Bingo, den? Orr . . . just look at her little

*face. She understands every word I say, don't you, Bingo?
Poodles are very intelligent dogs. A lot brighter than that
stupid whippet you wanted.*

An hour later, with mama-in-law sulking in injured
silence in the back of the car, Peregrine being quietly
sick, little Angela picking her nose and Bingo slob-
bering in father's ear, the family sets off. Stopping
only fourteen times on the way to answer the calls of
nature, rearrange the plastic boxes in the boot, fill the
radiator, and carry mama-in-law into a garage with
toilet facilities extensive enough to cope with her
permutation of problems.

At last the car arrives at the river.

*Right. Everybody out. Peregrine and Angela, you carry the
plastic boxes. You—yes, you, Cloth Ears—take the deckchairs, the rugs, the grip and the primus stove. You stay there
with Bingo, mother, until we've got everything sorted out.*

The procession moves along the bank, headed for
one of the best lies on the river, miraculously still
unoccupied.

*How much further do you think you're going? What do you
mean, we've only got another 400 yards to go? I don't care if
we've only got another 40 yards to go, I'm not having mother
traipsing all this way through these nettles. You know she's
got a bad leg. We'll stay here in the sun, where we can keep
warm. Get the deckchairs out, children, and start pumping the
primus. You can go back and collect mother and Bingo. Never
mind saying you've got to tackle up. You can tackle up later.
Go and get mother and do as you're told.*

The family makes camp on a spot on the bank
known to locals as Idiots' Reach. It is ideal for
deckchairs, primus stoves, cucumber sandwiches,
mothers-in-law and poodles. Its one drawback is that

only three fish have been caught there since records started.

Are we all settled then? Are you comfortable, mother? Never mind, love, I'll fill your bottie and then you'll feel a bit warmer. Peregrine and Angela, ask your father to get your rods ready for you. I don't like you messing about with all those hooks and maggots. What's that? If he gives you another thick ear he'll have me to reckon with. You go and tell him.

Eventually, mother-in-law stops groaning, Bingo stops rushing up and down the bank and concentrates on snuffling through the undergrowth, and even father gets tackled up and casts out. Silence descends on the river. Broken only by the click of knitting needles and:

So I said to her, I said, Mrs Johnson, I said, don't you take that attitude with me, I said. Two can play at that game, I said. You don't find my Albert up to those tricks, I said—oh! Peregrine's got his hook caught in the back of that man's neck. Go and help him to get it out. And tell him not to swear at Peregrine like that—he'll upset him . . .

. . . So I said to her, Mrs Johnson, I said—oh, stop it Albert! Why didn't you hit him back? Anybody would think a black eye was the end of the world.

. . . So I said to her, I said, looking her straight in the eye—she went white—I said, it wasn't my Albert who was thick with the barmaid at the Crown, I said. It wasn't him who was coming home every night with lipstick all down his shirt, I said.

Are you all right, mother? Have a good burp, dear, that'll help. No, I said, and the police weren't round at our house, after the washing disappeared off Mrs Fairclough's line, I said.

Angela! Stop eating those maids of honour like that! You'll be—oh, look at that mess! It was your clean blouse, too.

No, I said. And we know what was taken from that line, I said. I've read about people like that in the News of the—*Peregrine! Just be more careful! Now you go and help your father to get the hook out of his ear . . .*

The morning wears on. Fifteen times Father risks death and mutilation to bring Peregrine's tackle from surrounding trees. Fifteen times, in a shower of twigs, leaves and uptight birds.

A dozen times he has to duck to avoid being hooked by Peregrine's flailing tackle. Twice he is unsuccessful. And discovers a fellow feeling with the three other anglers whom Peregrine hooks. And allows them to remonstrate without protest.

Angela loses interest in the fishing altogether, eats five maids of honour, three eclairs, seven cucumber sandwiches, two scampi vol au vents, drinks half a pint of mushroom soup, spends half an hour skipping up and down the bank and is sick in the bait tin.

Bingo, tired by now of snuffling through the undergrowth, digs holes in the bank, steals sandwiches and barks at inoffensive anglers.

Mother-in-law complains that she is hungry, thirsty, too hot, too cold, that the sun's gone in, that the sun's come out, that her leg's gone dead, that her wind's coming on again, that the midges are biting, that there's an earwig in her cress sandwich and that she can't see the sense in a grown man just sitting there hour after hour doing nothing.

And as the noonday sun stands high in the sky . . .

Eighty four pence he tried to charge me for a piece of meat you could wrap in a postage stamp, 'If you think I'm paying that,' I said, 'you've got another think coming,' I said. Angela—stop feeding those maggots to the swans. You'll make them ill. Peregrine! Don't lean so far over that bank! Peregr—Now come out of there and get those wet clothes changed at once!

Albert! Where do you think you're going? Oh no, you're not! You don't think I went to the trouble of making all this orange squash to have you go gallivanting off to swill beer all lunchtime. You just stay—don't you dare call me that in front of mother! And what to mother? I've never been so . . .

Later that afternoon, tired, but thoroughly miserable, the family party makes its way back to the car. Mother-in-law's legs have seized up and her heartburn is giving her gyp. Peregrine is sniffling from a combination of one ducking and four thick ears. Angela is sniffling from a combination of hay fever, violent stomach ache, nettle rash and midge bites. Bingo slobbers in dad's ear. Dad's lunchtime anaesthetic has worn off and his expression is that of Genghis Khan on a bad day. But nothing is allowed to halt the flow:

. . . That was a fine place to take us, I must say. All that mud and those midges. And the language coming from those men up the bank. Not that you were setting any kind of example. I never thought I'd hear words like that coming from you. You're not still in the army, you know. I used to think you were such a quiet lad before we got married. Mind you, mother used to say that the quiet ones were the worst. I should have listened to her. What, mother? I said I should have listened to you . . . about him. You always said he had a shifty look . . . I wouldn't care if we'd caught any fish. Not a one. And all these years you've been coming home telling me how well you've done. I think it's just been the excuse for a glorified booze-up. Yes, mother, yes, shifty you said. You did love, yes, . . .

As Gilhooley once put it:

> *A family that angles together*
> *Sthrangles together.*

CHAPTER ELEVEN

Rules Of The Game

The need for rules and regulations is evident in every facet of our everyday life, and nowhere more evident than in the running of an angling club.

The number of rules varies enormously from club to club, with some clubs having so few restrictions that anyone would think they were concerned only with allowing anglers to enjoy themselves.

As Seamus Gilhooley has pointed out in his excellent volume, *Law and Order by the Waterside* (Plumduff and Spottidick £15.75, hardback £47.50), this can lead only to anarchy, violence, permissiveness and self indulgence.

Mr Gilhooley has himself formulated a set of rules which can stand as a model of comprehensiveness and clarity, and which he has kindly allowed me to reproduce in the following pages.

The rules, based on his own intensely practical experience as the founder, chairman, secretary and treasurer of a chain of angling clubs up and down the country, cover every possible eventuality.

Mr Gilhooley's clubs had their inevitable teething troubles. There were complaints from members that some of the waters turned out to be filled-in gravel pits or opencast mines, that some were situated on War Department property in the middle of artillery training ranges, that some could be reached only after a three-day pony trek through the remotest Cairngorms, and that others—which *did* hold water and were relatively easy of access—failed to yield any fish.

As Mr Gilhooley pointed out in his foreword:

'Once you allow yourself to be affected by the negative attitudes of the moaners and groaners, you cease to be a positive force for the betterment of the human condition.

'If I had thought as they did, I would never even have considered working day and night, through the best years of my life, to build up a chain of waters which, potentially, could give pleasure to millions. Once I have implemented the improvements now made possible through a government grant awarded to me by a grateful nation, there will be no possible cause for complaint.

'Meanwhile, I do not propose to allow a vociferous rabble to rampage all over my waters and give me nothing but abuse in return. My rules are designed to ensure that, come what may, the waterside will be a fit place for decent people to disport themselves in. So long as they watch how they are disporting.'

Rules

1. *Fishery permits*
Members must carry with them at all times a current permit, membership card, National Health card, certificate of vaccination, passport and blood sample. Failure to produce any of these at the request of a bailiff or other authorised person could result in a punch up the throat.

2. *Access to waters*
Access to fisheries is by the authorised entrance only. Members must not walk on standing crops, leaning crops, pasture land, ploughed land, seeded land, mown land, woodland, scrubland, downland or upland. The use of footpaths across any of the aforementioned areas is strictly forbidden.

Failure to comply with the above conditions will result in access being denied.

3. *Permitted hours*

Fishing is permitted from sunrise to sunset, except where entrance to the fishery is not permitted until later than sunrise, and departure from the fishery is insisted on before sunset.

The times listed above are subject to the exceptions of Christmas Day, Boxing Day, New Year's Day, Easter Monday, Good Friday, August Bank Holiday, St George's Day, St Andrew's Day, St Patrick's Day and Yom Kippur, when no fishing of any kind is allowed.

Fishing from Monday to Friday is not allowed. Weekend fishing is strictly prohibited.

Night fishing is banned on all waters. Day fishing is allowed only at the times stated above, subject to any change of policy not heretofore notified.

Persistent fishing outside the permitted hours could result in the hours being curtailed.

4. *Tackle*

A person shall use one rod and one line with one hook only providing these are not used in combination or at one and the same time.

Hooks may be of any pattern but the following: round bend, crystal, model perfect and any permutation of these as eyed, spade-ended or affixed ready-made to gut or nylon.

Lines must be of material other than cotton, flax, gut, silk, nylon or other artificial fibre, and must be of a method of manufacture other than monofilament or braided.

Reels can be anything other than fixed spool, centre pin, closed face or multiplier.

Any member found using one or a combination of these pieces of tackle, or anything else which takes the bailiff's fancy, stands liable to suffer confiscation of the offending article. Replacements may be purchased from any branch of Gooligear Ltd. Best prices paid for secondhand tackle. Special terms for bailiffs.

5. *Language*
Members must at all times behave in a gentlemanly manner. The use of foul language is expressly forbidden. Permitted words and phrases are 'Oh dear', 'Tut', 'Blow', 'Gunjy gumdrops' and 'Yah boo sucks'. Beyond these expletives, no others are to be used on club waters.

Any member discovered using prohibited words under his breath, even in moments of extreme stress, annoyance or peril, is liable to have his mouth washed out with soap and his name put in the Naughty Book.

6. *Fires*
No lighting of fires is allowed on the bank. Any angler who burns down a barn, haystack, standing crop, farmhouse or outbuildings thereof, does so at his own risk and will be personally responsible for explaining the situation to the farmer.

7. *Camping*
Camping is expressly forbidden, as is any kind whatsoever of eccentric or mincing walk, or the wearing of any item or items of apparel or jewellery likely to cause a breach of the peace.

8. *Litter*
No litter is to be left on the bank. Plastic bags, nylon line, cigarette packets, holed wellington boots, long johns, laddered tights or knickers must be taken home.

9. *Alcoholic liquor*
No alcoholic liquor is to be taken to, or consumed at

or by, the waterside. Anyone found in an inebriated condition, causing a disturbance, singing questionable songs or falling in, will be taken home immediately and propped against his front door without notice or explanation to anyone who may be in the house at the time. The club cannot accept responsibility for any domestic friction arising therefrom.

10. *Animal life*
No angler shall kick, beat, prod, belabour, abuse, project missiles at or otherwise interfere with or upset any swan or duck, or incite any other angler so to do.

The prodding or bashing of cows, bullocks, heifers or bulls with anything but the right forefinger or the Gilhooley Combined Cow Prodder and Basher (price £32.50, patent applied for) is strictly forbidden.

11. *Domestic Animals*
With certain exceptions, domestic animals or pets are not allowed at the waterside. The exceptions include certain fish, mammals and reptiles whose natural habitat is in or by the water, such as goldfish, alligators and dugongs. These may be allowed to take exercise in the water, on a lead and under proper supervision, providing that the club is not held responsible for any damage to:

(*a*) the goldfish, by perch, pike, kingfisher or other
predators;

(*b*) other anglers, by the alligator or dugong.

Any alligator or dugong which slips its collar must be reported immediately to the river authorities, the police, the RSPCA and the local open-air bathers' association.

12. *Calls of Nature*
It is a serious offence for members to use any farm building, shed, pump house, barn, hayloft, pigsty,

Any member in extremis *may be permitted* . . .

silage pit or moored or passing boat or barge, as a latrine.

Any attempt to use the water itself for such a purpose will be liable to prosecution under the Statute of 1397, Ordinances Against Unlawful Piddling By Ye Peasantry. Maximum penalties under this statute are 30 years' imprisonment, a fine of 15 groats, or hanging by the toes during the Queen's Pleasure.

Any member *in extremis* may be permitted, with the consent of other anglers present, to relieve himself in thick undergrowth, nettle beds or heavily wooded hollows. No aiming at passing flies, or any other form of diversion or exhibitionism, is allowed. Dress must be adjusted before leaving.

13. *Earthworks*
Digging of the banks for worms, the making of mud pies, the building of sand castles, or any form of opencast or vertical or horizontal shaft mining is forbidden.

14. *Unlawful methods of fishing*

No angler is allowed to use any automatic striking device, harpoon, sonar or radar tracking equipment, electrical underwater stunning device, seine net, carbide, gelignite, TNT or hand grenade, no matter how disappointing the results of fishing by conventional methods may have been.

15. *Entertainment*

No radios or portable television sets are allowed at the waterside. The playing of guitars, violins, banjos, mouth organs, double basses, drums, kazoos, comb and paper, or any other form of wind, string, percussion or electronic instrument is prohibited.

Any member discovered organising glee clubs, string quartets, concerts, talent shows, strip shows or love-ins, to the distress and inconvenience of other anglers, will be reported forthwith to Equity, The Lord's Day Observance Society and Mrs Mary Whitehouse.

16. *Security*

Members are forbidden to show copies of, or to discuss, these rules with the Press, police, other anglers, wives, fiancées, mistresses or anyone not included in these categories. Nor must the rules be perused in a public place, park, thoroughfare, public service vehicle, or anywhere other than in complete privacy behind locked doors. After being read, marked and learned, they should be eaten and inwardly digested.

17. *Miscellaneous*

Anything not covered by the above is strictly, absolutely and totally forbidden, prohibited and banned.

CHAPTER TWELVE

The Perils Of Angling

Like every other rugged, adventurous outdoor pursuit, angling is beset with perils and dangers that would daunt any ordinary man, but which merely give the angler a further incentive to press home the battle against raging elements and fierce, brute beasts.

The angler is cast in the classic mould. Where would we be, for instance, if it were not for men like Columbus, Raleigh, Drake, Frobisher, Hawkins, da Gama, Arthur, Nelson, Churchill and Gilhooley?[1]

Who but the angler, long inured to danger and pain, could shrug them off with sentiments akin to those expressed by Sherpa Tensing when, on the summit of Everest, Hillary accidentally stuck the flagpole up his nose?[2]

Alone he braves the elements, clad simply in two string vests, one pair of long johns, an army surplus shirt, three pullovers, one pair of pyjama trousers, one pair of battledress trousers, one pair of waterproof overtrousers, two pairs of socks, one pair of seaboot stockings, a pair of wellington boots, an ankle-length anorak, a bobbly hat and a nose cosy.

His only other sources of warmth and comfort are a collapsible windbreak, a six-foot umbrella, a camping stool, a foot muff, a hand warmer, two thermos

---

[1] I don't know. Ed.

[2] 'Do dat again, ya clumsy great shpalpeen an' Oi'll shplatter ya. (Freely translated by Gilhooley from the original Tibetan.)

His only other sources of warmth and comfort . . .

flasks, a plastic boxful of cheese and onion butties, a portable-television and a bottle of the hard stuff.

He goes out into the unknown, an epic figure with a sense of his own destiny, knowing only that a man has to do what he has to do. Now and again he does it. Discreetly. And taking care to avoid the nettles.[3]

The perils facing this man are many. It is only by being constantly on his guard that he can return to his

---

[3]See also under 'Gnats'.

loved ones unscathed. What follows, in an attempt to cut down the number of anglers who come home scathed, is a review of the most common dangers and ways of dealing with them. As the old proverb puts it, 'Forewarned is enough to put anybody off.'

Silly Old Moos

The most widespread hazard is the common domesticated cow. The most strenuous efforts by NaSAC (the National Society for the Abolition of Cows) have failed to make much impression on their numbers. Even a solitary specimen, however innocent looking, presents a potential hazard to health, life and limb.

Points of Recognition

Cows come in four different types:

1. Cows
2. Heifers
3. Bulls
4. Bullocks

Identification is important if avoidable complications are not to set in at a point where it is difficult to do anything about them.

All four have the same basic identification points: a tail with a tuft at the end, a leg at each corner and a head which carries a pair of horns and a gormless expression.

A *cow* can be recognised by her udders which are slung between the hindquarters and look like a water-filled rubber glove or a pair of plastic bagpipes, depending on whether the animal is a B or a C cup. The udders are where the milk is kept. (This is for the benefit of town anglers who think it comes from a machine outside the grocer's.)

A *heifer* is a teenage cow, and can be differentiated by her Junior Miss udders and expression of trusting virginity.

A *bull* is a different kettle of tea, not to say cup of fish. In place of udders he has a rather enviable set of what used to be described as wedding tackle. His expression can range from bleary to ferocious, depending on his luck, and he generally wears a ring through his nose.

A *bullock* is something which would have grown into a bull if his prospects had not been nipped in the bud. He can be recognised by his lack of recognisable points, pained expression and high-pitched moo. A bullock with long legs and no horns is likely to be a horse.

Watch Your Step

The most common hazard from all four kinds is the cow pat. This can be avoided during daylight by the simple expedients of stepping round or leaping over, and identified in the dark—unfortunately only when the damage has been done—by its soggy feeling and gentle squelching sound.

There are other circumstances in which a cow pat cannot be avoided; i.e., when it is, as it were, delivered. One of the prime reasons for Gilhooley's formation of NaSAC was because of one such unhappy circumstance.

One day he was unwise enough to lie down for forty winks on a bank after making no impression at all on the fish but a big one on a bottle of Power's.

Along came a cow, grazing absent-mindedly, which absent-mindedly did something very anti-social. All over Gilhooley. He was speechless (having been brought up never to speak with his mouth full).

In his NaSAC manifesto, Gilhooley lists many other anti-social activities of which cows are guilty, and devotes a chapter to defensive measures which the angler can adopt. A summary is as follows:

Blocking Roads

Cows are always getting out of their fields *en masse* and blocking roads. This can lead to slippery patches, dangerous to the motorist, and to the squashing of individual anglers trying to get into the field.

The motorised angler can attempt to unblock the road by putting his foot down and closing his eyes. The angler on foot or bicycle can do no better than to use the Gilhooley Combined Cow Prodder and Basher (patent applied for), price £32.50 from all good angling shops, agricultural suppliers and herbalists.

Damaging Things and Frightening People

Cows are always damaging anglers' equipment by walking on it, sitting on it, eating it or getting anti-social with it. In one year alone:

27,000	rod rests were bent beyond straightening
25,748	tins of maggots were kicked over or stood on
7,539	cheese and pickle butties were eaten
3,000	night-fishers' tents were scratched against
2,356	of these tents collapsed
1,974	night-fishers were trodden on
739	night-fishers were frightened out of their minds by being breathed on or mooed at in the dark

37 anglers were fallen on by cows which missed their footing at the top of the bank

23 of these anglers did themselves a mischief by misguidedly trying to get the cow up the bank again

1 angler was anti-socialled on, and NaSAC estimates that at least 20,000 more cases of this went unreported

This is obviously an intolerable situation and one against which we must pull up our socks and make a firm stand. With the help of the Gilhooley Combined Cow Prodder and Basher (patent applied for), price £32.50, we can perhaps see the bend in the road and the light at the end of the tunnel.

Cows' Nasty Diseases

Cows are always having really nasty diseases. To name but a few:

Anaplasmosis, Anthrax, Bang's Disease, Blackleg, Bloat, Botfly, Foot and Mouth, Lumpy Jaw, Mange, Rinderpest, and Texas Fever.

Having these nasty things often means that farms are sealed off and the waters declared out of bounds to anglers. Any angler found near these waters is liable to be stripped off and dumped in a trough of sheep dip. Which is a bit mean.

Any cows displaying symptoms of the above diseases must first be dealt a swift prod and bash with the Gilhooley Combined Cow Prodder and Basher (patent applied for), price £32.50; and then reported to the sanitary man. An angler who has been in contact with a diseased cow must go straight home, put a match to his clothes and soak himself in a bath of Jeyes' Fluid for 24 hours. Alternatively, soak his clothes in Jeyes' Fluid and put a match to himself.

Bulls Chasing People

In conditions of early morning mist or cases of severe hangover, the sex of an animal can be difficult to determine until the distance has closed so much that negotiation is out of the question.

A cow or a heifer can be shooed, prodded or bashed. A bullock can be reduced to a state of acute embarrassment by a cry of 'Moosy-woosy.'

But a bull needs sterner treatment. Even the Gilhooley Combined Cow Prodder and Basher (patent applied for), price £32.50, can prove to be but a flimsy defence and can be severely bent (replacement prodder blade, £12; replacement basher head, £13).

What is called for here is the Gilhooley Anti-Bull Three-Stage Master Plan. The stages can be worked in any permutation or sequence or used individually, according to the circumstances and urgency of the situation.

Stage One. Stand your ground. Look the bull straight in the eye (or both eyes if you can manage it) and impose your iron will on him. Within seconds he should be a grovelling, whimpering wreck.

Stage Two. If this fails, pick yourself up and apply the Gilhooley Japanese Horn Lock. Grab the bull's left horn in your left hand. Throw the right arm under the bull's neck and grasp the right horn firmly. With a deft flick, throw him over your right shoulder. Then, pinning him to the ground with both hands, tickle him somewhere strategic with the toe of your wellie. Once he is helpless with laughter, make good your escape.

Stage Three. Should the bull prove not to be the ticklish type, pick yourself up again, turn smartly about and divest yourself of the top article of clothing. Throw this on the ground for the bull to investigate, then make off at a swift but dignified trot.

Be ready to throw down another piece of clothing if he follows. And another, and another, until you can vault to safety over the nearest stile. Remember always to make for the *nearest* exit.[4]

After thanking Mr Gilhooley for the foregoing extract from his Manifesto, we can now turn to other angling perils.

Swansong

Swans are another of Nature's little jokes. Apart from sploshing around and scaring every fish for miles, they assume that the tins of bait and packets of butties have been brought specially for them by the RSPCA Meals on Wheels service.

If normal methods of persuasion (a clout with the landing net, a gentle pat with a brick) fail to dissuade them, try imitating the hunting call of the Upper Mersey Swan-Eating Seal (recordings available from Gilhooley Enterprises price £14.95 each, plus postage).

A last resort is the Bolton Swan Upping. This differs in many respects from the Thames Swan Upping, but is nonetheless hallowed by tradition.

A trail of chopped black pudding is laid from the water's edge to a convenient spot in front of a bush. Behind the bush, dressed in ratting cap and pit clogs, the Upper lies in wait.

The swan follows the trail, gobbling up the black pudding, and finishes, all unsuspecting and head

---

[4]Gilhooley once made the regrettable mistake of taking the long way round and was picked up on the motorway wearing a string vest and one sock. 'There's too much of this about,' said the magistrate.

down, in front of the bush. Out leaps the Upper and, with the traditional cry of 'Gerroopyabooger!' lifts the swan smartly in the air with the toe of his clog.

It was said of Elkanah Broadbottom, champion Upper of pre-war years, that he could shift a swan from Bolton to Bradford in his bare feet. Given good clogs and a ten-yard run up, he could have put Orson Welles on top of Manchester town hall with nothing but a bent toecap to show for it.

Gnats

Gnats, the minuscule curse of the water's edge, are particularly attracted to the subtle aura of the angler. They cannot resist the blend of old fish, cheese butty, draught bitter and venerable socks.

They can be kept at bay with a mixture of Wintergreen, sump oil and hydrochloric acid smeared liberally over the angler's exposed extremities. There is the danger here, however, that after two or three applications the angler might not have any extremities to expose.

Less drastic is the building of a smudge fire. By using fuel such as damp leaves, shredded tram driver's gloves, toenail parings and minced long johns, a particularly pungent smoke can be raised. So long as he keeps his head in the pall of smoke, the angler is perfectly safe from attack. It has been estimated that the use of a smudge fire each by 150 anglers along a one-mile stretch of canal bank for eight hours would result in the death of 3,758,435 gnats. And 150 anglers.

The real danger from gnats, however, comes when the call of Nature has to be answered. Gilhooley was once bitten by a gnat in a place not normally exposed to the elements. As the day wore on, the bite began to swell until the affected part assumed monstrous proportions.

On the way home he showed it to friends in the pub who were so convinced of his imminent demise that he did not have to pay for a drink all night. Still the swelling went on. When Gilhooley arrived home, hardly able to stand from the pain, he showed it to his wife, who fainted on the spot.

'Oi can't understhand it at all, at all,' said Gilhooley later. 'You'd think the woman had never seen a swollen kneecap before.'

• . . . So, before answering Nature's call by the river bank, arm yourself with a swatter. Use it with extreme caution and as little force as is compatible with efficiency.

Wasps

Wasps are another danger to health and composure. A proven way of trapping them is to place an old jamjar, smeared with jam and half full of water, on the bank by your side. The wasps will go for the jam, fall in the water and drown.

Be sure you remember that the jamjar is there. Another of Gilhooley's misfortunes befell when, in the excitement of playing a hard-fighting gudgeon, he picked up the jamjar in mistake for his pint pot.

'Dat's what Oi *call* beer,' he was heard to say as he was lifted into the ambulance. 'Got a boite to it loike a Connemara mule, so it has.'

Chills

The vagaries of the British climate are responsible for the queues of goose-pimpled anglers in doctors' waiting rooms every Monday morning. Any sport which

Another danger to health and composure . . .

keeps its participants out of doors through the whole of an English summer's day, with its usual mixture of hail, rain, sleet, snow, fog, frost, khamseen, mistral, haboob and Scotch mist, is bound to have its martyrs. But chilling is avoidable if the necessary precautions are taken.

First, check your clothing. Never cast a clout. Or

anything else. More than one seasoned angler has gone to the great peg draw in the sky because he left off one of his vests.

Secondly, look after the inner man. Have a good breakfast before you leave home. It need be nothing elaborate: eggs, bacon, sausages, fried bread, tomatoes, toasted cheese, potato cakes, liver, onions, beans, cabbage and ribs, fish fingers, black pudding, faggots and bubble and squeak should see you through until you can open your sandwiches.

Do not neglect to have a couple of good mugs of tea, liberally laced with rum or whisky. Better still, a couple of mugs of rum or whisky liberally laced with tea.

At the water's edge, set out your tackle so that everything can be reached without your having to move from the spot. Put up the windbreak, lash the umbrella to the top of it, lay down the groundsheet, set up your stool, put your feet in the foot muff, cover your knees with a travelling rug, put up the hood of your anorak and make sure your nose cosy fits snugly. Every half hour, or as often as is deemed necessary, take a tot of something to keep up the inner glow.

At opening time, when the fish will have stopped biting, move into the nearest pub and stay close to the fire. When the fish come on again, which is generally about half an hour after closing time, go back to the water and fish until the evening opening hour. This time, because of failing light, pack up your tackle and take it with you.

When you leave the pub at the end of the evening, keep in mind the importance of a good warm bed. Get into it as soon as you can. Do not bore your beloved with tales of the day's fishing; restore your circulation with some passionate lovemaking. Then wrap up well for the journey home.

Dehydration

This, fortunately, is a condition so rare among anglers that it scarcely deserves a mention. Symptoms are dryness of the throat, singleness of vision, clarity of speech, wholesomeness of complexion, a disinclination to brawl in public places, a shining ring of bright silver light hovering about four inches above the head, and a sneaking feeling that you are missing something.

Psychological Aberrations

One of the most insidious hazards of a day's fishing is the possible psychological effect. Being wrapped up in so many layers of clothing, staring for hours at a tiny float, and perhaps over-compensating for early symptoms of dehydration, can have certain disorientating results. Deprived of sensory perception through the normal channels, the brain becomes susceptible to all kinds of hallucinatory phenomena.

The most common of these is that the canal bank becomes bathed in golden sunlight, that the cooling towers have been replaced by waving palms, that the towpath is covered with golden sand and exotic starfish. Along the path, dressed only in a couple of strands of seaweed, floats a person bearing a striking resemblance to either Miss Bardot or Miss Welch.[5]

Adjusting your loincloth and dropping your

[5]These two young ladies account for 96 per cent of the identifiable phenomena. There have been occasional sightings of Mrs Mary Whitehouse and the Dowager Lady Birdwood, but these have been so rare as hardly to affect the main symptoms of the condition.

shoulder bag of jungle fresh peanuts, you rise to greet her. Hand in hand, you leap gracefully over the sand, dive into the warm crystal water and—after you have knifed a man-eating shark and a couple of alligators—you leap back together through the surf for what promises to be something rather special.

At this point you are generally seized by a feeling of creeping cold. You find that your left leg has gone over the bank, your wellie is filling with water, the cooling towers have come back and Miss Bardot (or Miss Welch as the case may be) has disappeared.

Once the hallucination has ended, the only course of action left is to pack up and make for the nearest point of hospitality to take something for the after effects.

Here, you can observe the mass effects of sensory deprivation on your fellow anglers. These take the form of a refusal to believe the most obvious truths. You tell them, for instance, of the fight you had with the 20-lb pike on roach tackle; of the way you played it for seven hours until finally you turned its monstrous head to the bank. Of how it bit through the handle of the landing net, leaving you no alternative but to grab it by the tail. Of how it turned on you, chomped off the toe of your wader and, with a massive leap, splashed back into the middle of the lake.

You tell them this, a patent and irrefutable truth, and they stare incredulously—one of the first signs of incipient mass hysteria. After a few seconds one of them breaks into a giggling fit. Instantly they all join in. The air is full of inane comments like: 'What did it do then—stick its head out and blow a raspberry?', 'That wasn't a pike—you'd hooked the corporation's killer whale!' and 'Here—have some birdseed . . .

bloody good bait for flying fish!'

There are two ways of dealing with an outbreak such as this. You can hold up your hand and shout above the din: 'Drinks all round—on me!'

This will bring them to their senses immediately and ensure a reverential silence, broken only by gasps of astonishment and cries of awe and agreement, as you repeat the story.

The second method, though less effective, is cheaper. You simply ignore them and console yourself with the thought that they have once and for all forfeited any chance of hearing how you took thirty brace of rainbow trout in two hours from a disused stretch of the Manchester Ship Canal.

CHAPTER THIRTEEN

Setting Up

> *'Twas Christmas day in the chipshop.*
> *The fryer was inclined to muff it.*
> *He said, 'What shall I do with the rock salmon, lads?'*
> *And the customers answered, 'Stuff it!'*

The battle is over. On the bank lies the monster fish you have dreamed of for years. It would break your heart to throw it back; it must be preserved for posterity. But there are no witnesses around, and a photograph could never do it justice. There is only one answer: stuff it.

Stuffing, alas, is a dying art. The great stuffers of the past—Fred (Sage and Onion) Micklethwaite, Kapok Carnoustie and Ramjam McGinty—are no longer with us. All died on the job: Micklethwaite of sage rash after a heavy Christmas, Carnoustie of *delirium tremens* after a delicate operation on a performing flea, and McGinty of exhaustion after a rush job on a Blue Whale.

Mourn them as we will, we must face the fact that their techniques were of another age. Science and technology have overtaken them. In saluting them and their work, we must acknowledge that their products had about them a literal quality which tended to take the romance away.

What is needed today are techniques which will capture the spirit of the fish, the ethos of fishing, the soul of the angler. We are looking for an apocryphal, rather than a literal, truth; an extension of credibility rather than a flat statement of fact. We have to give the fish that little extra someting. Size.

Into the breach has stepped Mr Seamus Gilhooley. His patented techniques—*Stomp'n Stuff, Stretch'n Stuff* and *Stuff'n Patch*, to name but a few—were developed from hard experience and tested to the full during the time he ran the Gooligame Safaris on the Grand Union Canal.

'A FIVE FOOT PIKE OR YOUR MONEY BACK!' was his slogan. And the solvency of his big game safaris was entirely due to the fact that though a pike might have been a little less than five feet long at the time of capture (say, 1 foot, 11½ inches), it was well over the guaranteed size by the time he had finished with it.

If I may quote further from some of Mr Gilhooley's advertising literature:

> Be the envy of your friends!!!!!
> Save £££££££££s !!!!!
> *Men*—Do they sneer at you in the clubhouse???
>   Do other anglers kick sand in your groundbait???
>   Do they twist your swingtip??? Mangle your maggots???
>   Do pretty girls pooh-pooh your pike and giggle at your gudgeon???
>
> *BE THE FIRST IN YOUR STREET!!!!!*
> To have a three-foot roach!!!!!
>   A king-sized perch!!!!!
>   Reassure your wife!!!!!
>   Amaze your girl!!!!!
>   Impress your boss!!!!!
>   Terrify your friends!!!!!
> . . . *with a KING KONG PIKE!!!!!*

Let us, then, examine some of Mr Gilhooley's techniques in more detail, remembering before we start' the Golden Rule: make sure the fish is dead. Mr Gilhooley still bears on his nose the teeth marks of a very surprised pike. ('Dere's somethin' about bein' shtuffed dat dey don't loike at all,' he was reported as saying.)

Stomp'n Stuff

This technique is suitable for the deep-bodied fish, such as perch, tench and bream, where depth is as important as length.

Lay the fish on its side on several layers of newspaper. The *Daily Mirror* and the *Guardian* are recommended as having more absorbency than *The Times* or the *Daily Telegraph*. Place several more layers on top. Now place the wrapped fish on the floor.

Put on a pair of old army boots and, over them, several pairs of old socks. (The socks prevent damage to the fish by the studs and ensure a firmer foothold on the fish should the paper split.)

Now stand a pair of step ladders beside the fish. Mount the first step, turn to face the fish and, with feet together, hands by the side and thumbs in line with the seam of the trousers, jump.

Repeat this procedure from every step of the ladder. Then peel off the top layers of newspaper and inspect the fish. By this time it should be reasonably flat and roughly 2½ times its original area. Detailed stomping can now be carried out, with one or both feet, to fill out the natural curves.

The fish can now be gutted and cleaned. (After a really vigorous stomping this is often not necessary: the innards have simply to be scraped off the carpet.) Lovers of fish dishes can save the insides for a bouillabaisse.

The empty skin is filled with killed plaster of Paris and, after being allowed to dry, painted tastefully with oil paints or photographic tints and then varnished.

Stretch'n Stuff

In this method the fish is gutted first, packed with brewer's yeast, sewn up tightly and placed in a warm oven. After four hours or when the oven door bursts open, whichever is the sooner, the fish is taken out and the yeast replaced with plaster of Paris. (Save the yeast: it's good for spots.)

Should the scales of the fish have curled because of the heat, brush them with olive oil and run over them lightly with a medium-hot flat iron. Should the scales persist in curling, either squirt a little impact adhesive under each and iron again, or tack them down.

Alternative methods to the yeast treatment are:

(*a*) to stretch the skin over a wire coathanger or

(*b*) to stick in a shoe tree.

These methods, however, while having the advantages of cheapness, speed and cleanliness, have the drawback of making the finished job look like:

(*a*) Quasimodo's gardening jumper or

(*b*) an old clog.

Stuff'n Patch

This is the method used with so much success on pike. Ideally, for each pike one needs three more of roughly the same size. The first pike is cleaned and the skin cut vertically in half. The middle sections of the other three pike skins are then cut out and sewn between the head and tail sections of the first. The composite fish is now filled with plaster and the underside sewn up.

After the fish has been painted and varnished, the

'Nivver can ye tell the divvil a bit of difference . . .'

stitching may still be visible. This can be camouflaged in the mounting by strategically placed bits of foliage.

Should it so happen that only one pike is available, the amount of foliage can be increased to make a solid screen about 3 foot 6 inches long. The front and back halves of the pike are then mounted at either end of a piece of broomstick handle about 3 foot 4 inches long. The whole thing is placed behind the screen of foliage so that the front and back of the pike poke out at each end.

('Nivver can ye tell the divvil a bit of difference,' says Gilhooley. 'An' it's cheaper, too.')

CHAPTER FOURTEEN

The People You Meet

One of the biggest problems on the river bank is other people. To the casual wanderer, with nothing better to do, the angler is there for the specific purpose of being pestered, chatted up, argued with or borrowed from. Complete strangers think nothing at all of pawing through all of his personal belongings while rabbiting on about the weather, the state of the economy, the Common Market or the futility of an occupation which involves sitting for eight hours drowning worms.

He is approached by screwballs, layabouts, lurkers, peeping Toms, meths drinkers, religious maniacs, vegetarians, bovver boys, and old ladies with strong views on the dreadfulness of it all. Curiously, he is seldom approached by a beautiful nymphomaniac heiress whose father owns a brewery.

No matter how far away from human habitation the angler sits, it seldom takes longer than half an hour for a speck to appear on the horizon, homing in with the unerring accuracy of a moonshot. The angler cannot get away. The very immobility which the pursuit demands makes him the perfect target and gives him no opportunity or excuse for flight. The only defence is the verbal squelch. Most of us can think of it—but only ten minutes after the interrogator has gone.

The solution is to rehearse, to have the answers ready before the relationship becomes too involved. To this end, the Gilhooley Institute of Verbal Studies has issued a leaflet which lists the most common

The solution is to rehearse . . .

situations and offers instant verbal defence. I am
indebted to the Institute for permission to reproduce
the following paraphrase (after translation from the
original Liverpool Erse).

The old Lady

There is the old lady. About 70. Anti-vivisectionist.
Feeds stray cats and is accompanied by a fat and gentle
crossbred bitch. Apart from the out-and-out bovver
boys, she is the fiercest of the lot.

'You ought to be ashamed of yourself, a grown man like you! Inflicting pain on poor dumb creatures and setting such a dreadful example to every innocent child who happens to wander this way! How would you like to be impaled in the middle of your dinner, pulled off the streets and battered to death?'

The technique with this lovely old bat is to glance furtively about, put a warning finger to your lips, beckon her away from any vegetation which might contain special agents from the National Anglers' Council, and say in hushed and urgent tones:

'Madam—one never knows who may be watching. I'm actually a double agent from the League of Friends of Dumb Sticklebacks, taking part in a scientific study of the pain-threshold of cold-blooded aquatic vertebrates. With the evidence I hope to gather, we may be able to stamp out this diabolical pastime once and for all.

'For my work I need absolute quiet. I'm sure you understand—for the advancement of our common cause I have to be left strictly alone. And I should deem it a great favour if you did not mention my presence to any anglers you may meet on your way along the bank. If they so much as suspected what my mission really was, our whole enterprise could come to nothing.'

This is generally enough to have her fumble in her purse and press a pound note into your hand for the work of the League, before tiptoeing away with tear-dimmed eyes and a deep appreciation of your noble activities.

The Rising Generation

Inevitably, there is the mob of young thugs, snotty-nosed and out at elbow, who stampede along the bank and dive in a bunch upon your keepnet. They haul it out of the water and bellow in chorus:

'Cor, you ain't doin' so well, are you, mister. My dad/bruvver/uncle caught fahsands bigger 'n these last week. Wotcher bin doin' all day, dozy old git?'

The traditional answer used to be swift clip over the collective earholes. But in these days of child psychology and rapid communication, such an act can bring over the horizon in a matter of minutes the vast and menacing figure of dad/bruvver/uncle or policeman. So it is best to resort to a psychological technique long acknowledged for its effectiveness: bribery.

Depending on the size of the mob and how much you are in funds, a distribution of small change on the promise that they will disappear from your life forever should send them scuttling for the nearest ice cream stall.

The danger of this technique is that on the way they might meet another pack of delinquents and announce that the silly old git down the bank gave them all that money to clear off. Nothing is more certain to ensure that you will not lack company for long.

An alternative, but anti-social, technique is to tell them that you are fishing in a bad spot, but that a chap about half a mile downstream has caught so many pike, barbel, carp, barracudas and killer whales that the zoo is sending down a special tank to pick them up.

It's anti-social because it means that some other innocent angler will be lumbered with the little monsters. But you can salve your conscience with the thought that you would rather it were his problem than yours.

The Cadger

There's one to every stretch of water: the professional cadger who wanders along looking underprivileged and asks if you could possibly sell him some maggots/worms/cheese/breadpaste/cigarettes. Never *give*. Always *sell*.

Take him at his word. 'Certainly, old chap. Be glad to. I'm a bit low on the old maggots today, but I hate to see a man caught short. You can have 20 for two pence each, that's a quid. OK?'

Or you can try: 'Sorry, old chap. I'm almost out at the moment. But the bailiff has promised to bring me some: he should be along at any moment.'

As the bloke who has no bait generally has no licence either, he tends not to stick around for the bailiff.

The Bovver Boys

In their big boots, half-mast trousers, red braces and suede haircuts, they look for trouble from under their Peking Man foreheads. The trouble they can offer, depending on their communal ingenuity, can range from anything to tipping your maggots over your head to throwing all your gear—and finally you—into the drink.

Start on this lot before they start on you.

' 'Morning, lads. By heck, you're lucky—they've just gone back the other way. The police. Said they were looking for six well-built youths in connection with some trouble along the bank. No, I don't know any details (keep it vague as vague) but they seemed determined to get somebody for it.'

As you are unlikely to be the bovver boys' first customer of the day, they will probably clear off smartly. If they hesitate, or start eyeing up your gear for a dumping job before they leave, look at the whole bunch and say 'Ah yes, *you've* been in trouble before, haven't you'. The ones who *have* been in trouble will start guiltily and—with any luck—will lead the others down the bank at a swift trot.

The one possible danger of this approach is that it could misfire, leaving you and your tackle a bit damp. In which case the Gilhooley Institute for Verbal Studies offers its deepest sympathy and disclaims all responsibility.

The nice old Boy

The old boy who remembers a time on the river that never was (not in his lifetime, anyway) when worms were being tipped in by the sackful and barbel pulled out by the hundredweight, is really too nice to be given the straight brush-off. Even though he may be talking a load of absolute codswallop, he probably believes every word, and it would be a cruelty to disabuse him.

So you can tell him that you really regret the passing of those marvellous old days, that you are after the one big barbel left in the river, and that the next few minutes might see the realisation of twenty years of hoping and dreaming.

He will understand completely and will sit down, under your direction, in the wettest, windiest, coldest and most uncomfortable place on the bank, just so that he won't be a nuisance or get in the way.

After ten minutes his rheumatism will start playing him up and he will suddenly remember that it's time for his morning cocoa back home.

The dirty old Man

The sinister old boy (sometimes not so old) with the

long raincoat, silk scarf and shuffling walk, must be dealt with immediately and firmly. Poor old lad, his basic problem is loneliness and lack of love. But you are there to fish, not to play psychiatrist to every old kink who comes your way.

The danger with this old lad is that once he starts talking he is almost impossible to shut up. In the absence of any courting couples, he will stand behind you for a time, coughing politely to attract your attention.

After ten minutes or so of unheeded coughs, sniffs and shuffles, he will sigh and say, 'Ah, patience is a wonderful thing.' Answered or not, he will continue: 'I've always fancied fishing myself, very relaxing, I believe. And my doctor is always telling me to take it up. But I don't have the patience, not really. I was telling my doctor only the other day . . .'

Unchecked, he will wander through a detailed list of his symptoms and arrive, through some curious process of DOM logic, at the Problems of Young People Today. He will be seriously concerned about teenage sex, horrified at the spread of VD, aghast at see-through blouses and mini-skirts, appalled at the permissiveness in the cinema, on the stage and in the bookshops. Oh, horror. Oh, woe. And he'll enjoy every minute of it.

The only thing to do is to stop him before he gets into his stride. Ignoring him is useless. So is arguing, or pleading to be left in peace and quiet. So you say, with an occasional sniff and twitch:

'Yer, patience. That's wot the headshrinker said I needed. Fer me nerves, like. When I came out after me last stretch fer GBH, he told me ter take up fishin'. Stop me smashin' geezers up fer nuffin', like. I wouldn't care, but the last bloke I duffed over only needed 27 stitches. Nah, the bloke before that—he really *was* in a mess, I've got to admit it . . .'

By this time you should be talking to yourself, with the long raincoat doing a quick shuffle into the middle distance.

The Beautiful Nymphomaniac Heiress whose Father owns a Brewery

Say 'Yes'.

CHAPTER FIFTEEN

The Image Of The Angler

Coarse fishing has suffered for too long from a cloth cap image. The public at large tends to think of the angler as a rough-looking chap in wellingtons, raincoat and a flat cap, sitting on a canal bank swigging light ale from a bottle. This misconception has grown up because the angler generally is a rough-looking chap in wellingtons, raincoat and a flat cap, sitting on a canal bank swigging light ale from a bottle.

This image is doing him no good at all, even though he might be anything from a redundant dustman to a captain of industry or a brain surgeon.

It does him no good, for instance, when public money is being handed out. (Government funds, such as they are, for the improvement and maintenance of recreational waters, tend to be given more readily to schemes for making the waters fit for power boats and water skiers than to improving the angling facilities.)

It does him no good in the tarted-up 'fun' pubs of the waterside. While the weekend sailors are handed their halves of bitter and camparis and soda in a flurry of tugged forelocks, the anglers are greeted with the suggestion that they might be more comfortable in the public bar, in the garden, in the shed or in the pub down the road.

So the image must be changed. The angler must join the In Crowd, the Fun People, the trendy, dashing, handsome, young Colour Section swingers who appear in telly commercials going ecstatic over the taste of a fish finger or drooling over the silken sheen of a new toilet roll. Only then will it be realised that under the angler's drab exterior is an epic hero, a swashbuckler, every bit as dashing as the amateur sailor prancing about in his Mickey Mouse commodore's cap and blue blazer with the silver buttons.

A firm of specialist public relations consultants has come into being to deal with this very situation. Gooliplan, working on the basis of if-you-can't-beat-'em-join-'em, has launched a multi-million pence campaign to improve the angling image.

Gooliplan's PR techniques include television commercials, Press handouts, fashion shows, Angler-of-the-Year awards, and beauty contests for titles such as Miss Long Corker, Miss Stret Pegger and Miss Dough Bobbin.

The Gooliplan fashion shops, run under the name 'Goolitique', carry such special lines as anoraks with sergeant's stripes on the sleeves and gold epaulettes on the shoulders, bobbly hats with 'Boss Cat' embroidered across the front, rod holdalls made from lengths of plastic drainpipe with BAZOOKA printed in blood red on the side, fisherman's knives stamped with the name 'Jim Bowie' and wellingtons with 'These boots are gonna walk' on one toecap and 'all over you' on the other.

How does the angler look in all this? The rave reviews in the Press speak for themselves:

'Soopah!'—*The Sunday Times*

'A dolly man'—*Honey*

'A rugged rogue'—*Vogue*

'A dogfish's dinner'—*Tailor and Cutter*

'Bloody ridiculous'—*The Wigan Observer*.

'Oi have ter admit,' says Mr Seamus Gilhooley, chairman and managing director of Gooliplan, 'dat ye can't actually *fish* in dat lot. But ye can walk down de King's Road, Chelsea, wid yer head held hoigh.'

One of the first problems to be tackled by Gooliplan was the relations between anglers and weekend sailors. The tendency of powerboat men, for instance, to cut a swathe through a row of fishing lines and to set up a wash that undercuts banks restored by public money, has often led to a mutually uncomplimentary exchange of views.

The Gooliplan Manual, *The Compleat Angler*,[1] includes a section on language, tactics and behaviour to be used in this kind of confrontation. It points out that not only is the choice of words of the utmost importance, but so, too, is their delivery.

The traditional vocabulary is out. Phrases such as, 'Sod off, you fascist pig!' have been so overworked on children's television programmes that they have lost almost all their former impact. Nor is the use of a working-class accent the deterrent it used to be since television producers, budding novelists and advertising art directors started taking elocution lessons to acquire one.

Phrases no longer recommended, apart from those already mentioned are:

'Do that again and I'll clog you rotten.'—(He would not know a clog if he saw one, and therefore could never conceive the state of being clogged rotten.)

'Tell that wench to put some clothes on.'— (Most powerboat men seem to have a blonde built into the back of the boat. As she seldom seems to wear anything more than a couple of see-through bootlaces, any reference to this is wasted on empty air.)

'Get away from my line, you chinless, pimply-

---

[1] The title *The Compleat Angler* is the brainchild of Mr Gilhooley. 'Oi thought of lots more,' he said, 'but dis one won on sheer originality.'

faced reactionary git.'—(Nobody ever thinks of himself as chinless, pimply-faced or reactionary, let alone a git. The chinless, pimply-faced reactionary git would be looking around to see who was being shouted at.)

'Don't walk through Salford after dark, lad—I'll have yer.'—(His presence in Salford either after dark or in broad daylight, on foot or otherwise, is so unlikely as to render this threat completely ineffective.)

The recommended method of dealing with approaching power boats is to carry a megaphone, don a peaked cap, make some ostentatious scribbles in a notebook and use one of the following:

'Ahoy there! You are holed below the waterline. Be so good as to reduce speed to three knots, tie up at the next landing stage and await the arrival of the salvage crew.'

'Ahoy there! You are reported to have exceeded the speed limit. A uniformed constable awaits you at the next moorings.'

'Ahoy there! The Spring/Summer/Autumn/Winter bore is approaching at a height of approximately twelve feet. Please tie up at the next moorings and make all speed to a place of safety.'

Should the angler feel confident enough in his own physical prowess, or at least in his ability to bluff, he could try something like:

'Excuse me, old chap. If you do not reduce speed this instant, I shall be obliged to board you and perhaps tear your ears off.'

'I hesitate to mention this, but I am both a county swimming champion and a Judo Black Belt. If you do not take that craft out of the immediate vicinity I shall board you and do something rather nasty to your more vulnerable parts.'

The presence of a girl in the back of the boat offers other opportunities:

'Ahoy there, madam! Will you please adjust your clothing! The River Authority's Ladies' Section has registered a strong complaint to the Committee.'

Addressed to the man:

'Ahoy there! Your wife is waiting for you at the clubhouse.'

Should he reply that the lady on the boat *is* his wife—an unlikely circumstance—respond with: 'Well, the lady at the clubhouse says that *she* is your wife. You'll recognise her easily enough—the pregnant one.'

Should one not be looking one's best, and be bereft of peaked cap and megaphone, wave a bottle of gin and shout drunkenly at the girl in the roughest possible accent:

'Come 'ome, our Ada! Ah can't manage them four kids on me own . . .'

The use of missiles to deter craft, or to remonstrate after the severing of fishing lines, is unfortunately a frequent happening. Gooliplan, while acknowledging the provocation that leads to the throwing of missiles, condemns their use on the grounds of (*a*) lack of sophistication and (*b*) lack of effectiveness.

The lack of effectiveness is demonstrated by the statistics for missiles launched at passing boats between June 16, 1981, and March 14, 1982:

Missiles	*Number Thrown*	*Number on Target*
Bottles (empty)	16,741	7
Bottles (full)	4	1
Bricks	14,389	3
Maggot tins	5,483	2
Rod rests	2,459	5
Wellington boots (right)	1,475	2
Wellington boots (left)	3,794	6

The discrepancy in the number of full and empty bottles thrown is attributable to the fact that, (a) at any given time, more are likely to be empty than full and (b) anglers are loath to part with a full one except in moments of unbearable stress and provocation.

The discrepancy in the number of left and right wellington boots thrown is accounted for by the fact that three out of every four anglers take off their left boot before the right.

The relatively high proportion of successful hits with rod rests is attributable to the javelin shape of the longer versions. A sub-committee of the Geneva Convention has been meeting for thirty-five years to consider banning their use.

Passive Resistance

Gooliplan suggests that a policy of passive resistance might be more effective than physical violence. Most of the confrontations need never take place if a little time were spent at the moorings before the boats were due to set out for the day. Half an hour with swimming trunks and a ¾ in. drill can work wonders.

The Longer View

While offering solutions to the short-term problems, Gooliplan is not neglecting the future. A concentrated PR campaign is ensuring that the Press is fed daily with stories about angling and anglers. The reading public is being educated to the fact that the angler is a responsible, valuable and much-loved member of society.

Who can forget, for instance, such headlines as:

Angler's Sister's Daughter-in-law Has Quins
Anglers Say No to Soaring Costs

. . . and many, many others?

One story which really showed what the angler is made of was the following, reproduced, with grateful acknowledgement, from the *Sludgethorpe Echo*:

ANGLER SAVES BARMAID IN PUB INFERNO

Angler Horace Wimpole (53), of the Clinker Lane Waltonians, Sludgethorpe ('I go fishing every Saturday and Sunday, come rain or shine') was the hero of a blaze at the Bricklayer's Arms last night.

A fire which broke out in the Snug spread quickly to the Saloon Bar. Braving flames and suffocating smoke, Horace dashed into the Saloon and carried out barmaid Esme Pringle (23).

After giving Miss Pringle the kiss of life in the shrubbery outside, he rushed back into the Saloon Bar and salvaged eight bottles of whisky, seven bottles of gin, three crates of brown ale and a stuffed pike, before he was beaten back by the flames.

'It was nothing, really,' said Horace. 'Angling keeps you on your toes, ready for any emergency.'

Two people died in the fire: Mrs Matilda Wimpole (51) and her widowed mother, Mrs Emily Throngbody (75). Both were sitting near the source of the blaze.

'I shall miss Mrs Wimpole,' said Horace. 'She was always a good wife to me.'

Puffing at his pipe, Horace—an unemployed tramways engineer—described his lucky escape when the fire first broke out.

'It started in the Snug, right next to where I'd been sitting,' he said. 'I'd just knocked my pipe out and popped round to the gents when I heard the screams. If I'd still been sitting there I'd have gone up like a torch.'

Will the tragedy affect his plans for Saturday's match against Penstone Piscatorials?

'Not really. The funeral's at 11 o'clock, but the peg draw isn't until half past one, so I should be all right.'

His plans for the future?

'Hard to say, just at the moment. But I think I'll get married and settle down. Esme's a good girl. And with her wages and what I'll draw from the insurance, we should be able to manage.'

. . . So, for angling hero Albert—a happy ending after all.

Another Gooliplan story which made the front pages all over the world was of the occasion when two humble anglers came virtually face to face with Royalty.

QUEEN SEES ANGLERS

Her Majesty the Queen today visited Throcklington Vale to open the £200 million pumping station.

Just three-quarters of a mile away, at Throcklington Reservoir, Mr Frederick Wilkins (73) and his son, Cyril (51) were fishing for pike. It is believed that they were visible from the platform on which Her Majesty unveiled a stone tablet to declare the pumping station open.

The Queen was wearing a powder blue flowered hat, with a powder blue coat and accessories to match. Mr Wilkins snr was wearing an ex-GPO overcoat, off-brown trousers and black gumboots. Cyril favoured a government surplus gas cape and pit boots.

'The thrill of a lifetime,' chorused Frederick and Cyril when they were told the news. 'To think—if we hadn't been lifelong anglers, it might never have happened.'

A Buckingham Palace spokesman declined to comment.

The influence of the campaign can be seen also in the recent spate of novels with an angling theme. Take this extract, for instance, from *Gozzers Are Forever*, by Ian Robbins:

The scream was thin and high and cut through the mist like a laser.

Shuft knew at once. Pinkie Swingtip—would she never learn?

Dropping his 15-foot Milbro carbon fibre match rod, 00035 stuffed a shiny metal canister into the pocket of his mohair raincoat and jammed a powerful, telescopic rod rest through the top of his startlingly white seaboot stocking and down the inside of his olive-green wellington boot.

His wellingtons were built for combat. Ex-Pioneer Corps Ministry of Defence surplus. Low in the heel. Loose round the calf. Broad round the toe and rugged under the sole. A *man's* wellie, he thought, as he raced along the broken length of the towpath.

The mist made the going difficult. Every few yards the bank had collapsed, leaving a great gap filled with menacing green water. As Shuft found the holes, he leapt in great space-devouring bounds. Once he failed to make it.

Cursing as he emptied the evil-smelling slime from his wellingtons and wringing out his seaboot stockings, which by this time had turned a dirty khaki, he let his mind drift back to Pinkie. Whatever trouble she was in this time, he had to get her out. And fast. He owed her something. From the night of the Hotpot Supper after the Nene Championships.

The hotpot. Fried potatoes, sliced exactly at a thickness of 5/64ths of an inch. Aphrodisiacal rings of

Spanish onion, cut across the grain, no more than 3/64ths thick. Tender strips from the neck of a nine-year-old lamb. All laid lovingly in one-inch layers to the top of a deep earthenware dish, the colour of a fresh-ploughed field. Simmered for four hours. Shaken, not stirred. And ladled out with Big Jim's Victorian moustache cup.

They had sat, he and Pinkie, side by side on the stairs at Big Jim's. The plates on their knees. Forking together at the hotpot as the piano downstairs vibrated insistently, 'Ee-Ay-Addio, We've Won the Cup.'

The excitement in the air, the inner glow of the hotpot, the barbaric beat of the music. Together they had done something to Pinkie. She was no longer Miss Swingtip from Packing Bay Number Four at the biscuit factory. She was a woman. Primitive, unbridled, as only a woman can be. Lusting . . . as only a woman can lust.

Shuft had hesitated a moment before—unable to control himself any longer—his questing hand had found the bobble and pulled the woolly hat free from the curling golden hair with the tantalising mouse-brown roots. They had looked at each other for a fraction of a second which seemed eternity. Then two plates of hotpot had gone clattering down the stairs . . .

Another piercing scream jerked Shuft out of his reverie. God! What was he thinking of? He stopped thinking of it, pulled on his wellingtons and charged again down the towpath.

The sound of rushing water met his ears. A large dark shape loomed up, spanning the canal from bank to bank. The lock gates! Tied between them was Pinkie. Gad, thought Shuft, that's stretching it a bit. And there, turning the handle to open the gates, was

Swinish Swetto, the Serbian Stret-Pegger.

Shuft saw it all now. Humiliated by his defeat in the European Championships, aware that the Common Market was to bring hordes of Wigan match anglers to keep the big prizes out of his reach for ever, Swetto was taking a diabolical revenge.

'Stay right where you are. Right there.'

Shuft's voice held the menace well known to others who had crossed him in the crib school on social nights.

'Drop that handle or you are a dead Serb!'

'Aha!' screamed Swetto, garlic fumes gusting in waves from between his blackened teeth. 'Ze leetle Eenglish matchman, eh? Well you are no match for Swetto, my frien'. Nevair again will you fling your steenking soap into Swetto's swim. Nevair again will you 'ook 'im in ze back of ze neck. Now you die. And leetle Peenkie dies wiz you!'

Swetto advanced menacingly, the lock handle gripped in his great hairy hands. Shuft felt gingerly in his pocket for the canister, eased it out and loosened the lid. His fingers checked that the contents were still there. They were. Evil, squirming, like beings from the beginning of the world. He was almost sorry for Swetto.

The lock handle flashed down. Shuft deflected it with a swift flick of the rod rest and threw the contents of the canister into Swetto's face.

The Serb could not believe it at first. He tried to speak, but no words would come. His eyes signalled hate and horror. But he was past hating. Past loving. Past anything. With a mouthful of gozzers he fell back, spluttering, into the canal. One arm rose for a brief moment above the detergent foam, then disappeared.

The canal was quiet again. No movement, except

for the scuds of foam, lifted by a gentle breeze. No sound, except for the creaking of the lock gates and Pinkie.

With the handle, which Swetto had dropped as he fell, Shuft wound the lock gates shut. Swiftly he cut Pinkie free and hauled her to safety.

Tenderly he untied the ropes, and spent an interesting ten minutes wiping the silkweed from her bruised flesh.

She opened her eyes.

'Where,' she gasped, 'is Swetto?'

'Where he can trouble you no more, my love,' breathed Shuft.

'You swine!' Pinkie screamed. 'He was so masterful! Don't you understand? I love him, you great pimply Anglo-Saxon oaf!'

She snatched up the lock handle. It rose and fell. Just once. The mists closed back in over the towpath. Shuft's shattered head, once so handsome, lifted itself from the gravel.

'Dad was right,' it croaked. 'Women and fishing *don't* mix. I wish I hadn't wasted those bloody gozzers now. . .'

Finally, probably the greatest success of the campaign: the image-building television commercials, devised by Gooliplan to sell both angling and the angler.

The first two sold angling, and were designed mainly to encourage young men to take up the sport, a sport in which they could forget their problems of loneliness and real or fancied inadequacies. The others cast the angler in a recognisable identity mould.

The following examples should serve to illustrate the points:

The Canal-Fresh Angler

The commercial opens with a woman's voice singing:

> *There are two men in my life.*
> *One of them is my husband,*
> *The other daren't tell his wife.*
> *And they both have smelly feet. . .*

Then a friendly, but authoritative man's voice cuts in:

'Do you have smelly feet? Understains on your overshoes? The kind of feet it's difficult even to talk about?

'Then get them fresh again with the Great Outdoors. Go fishing, young man. Tramp through Mother Nature's soothing grass. Get the chlorophyll to your cuticles. Dabble your plates in the cooling waters of the Grand Union Canal. Get fresh with angling's secret ingredient—water.'

As this is being said, there is a scene of a distant house, high on a misty hill, whence walks a solitary, sad-looking man. At the window, watching him go, is the tear-stained face of his wife.

As the man walks through the grass, his step visibly lightens. He arrives at the water's edge, takes off his boots and socks, and dabbles his feet in the soothing water, a blissful smile spreading across his face. A little further down the bank, an angler is drying his feet and putting his boots back on. The angler rises and walks purposefully up the hill towards the house. The woman's face appears again at the window, this time aglow with anticipation.

The scene fades out, to the accompaniment of 'Some Enchanted Evening' and 'There'll be a Hot Time in the Old Town Tonight' . . .

The Irresistible Angler

A bespectacled, pimply youth sits sadly on the river bank, watching a procession of beautiful girls file past, each one completely ignoring him, each one with her eyes fixed on a distant figure seated further along the bank. Soon, the distant figure is surrounded by a clamouring crowd of women.

The pimply youth can stand it no longer. He rushes up to the crowd, fights his way through the ravening girls, and reaches the figure in the middle— another bespectacled, pimply youth.

'What have you got that I haven't got?' he pleads. 'Why do they all fight over you?'

'I've got this,' says the other youth, and picks up a fishing rod. At which the girls go completely berserk and fling themselves in a heap on top of him.

The scene fades out and then comes back again to the first pimply youth, this time sitting on the bank with a rod in his hand. Down from the bridge comes hurrying a long crocodile of squealing girls, heading straight for him.

'OK, kids,' he says, coolly. 'The line forms on the right . . .'

The Sex Symbol

He roars down the towpath of the Kennet and Avon in his get-away aubergine Mercedes. Out he leaps, followed by his Neanderthal bodyguard and posse of dolly birds in see-through kaftans and Oliver Goldsmith specs, pointing his rod at the chosen spot.

Everyone bounces in slow motion down to the pitch, with slim, manicured hands carrying rod rests, buckets of groundbait and tins of liver maggots.

With swift karate chops, the Neanderthal Man lays low every girl but one. Then the camera pans quickly to the top of the bank, where the morning sun slants significantly through the trees. The dolly girl is in full flight, still in slow motion, having lost her kaftan and making do with hot pants and clinging grandad vest. Angler leaps after her, moonwalkwise, in glistening golden wellies.

She stops. Turns. Reclines expectantly on a mossy hummock between the trees. He overtakes. Sinks down beside her. And dangles before her incredulous eyes . . . the most magnificent 3 oz 9 dram gudgeon you ever saw. As the scene fades she murmurs: 'I don't know much about fishing . . . but I like the men who do it . . .'

The Provident Angler

A luxury liner is going down in flames after a collision with an iceberg in a hurricane on the Trent. Panic everywhere as passengers throw themselves overboard without so much as a glance at the peg draw and starting prices pinned up on the funnel.

Everybody is berserking. Except the matchman. Methodically packing his gear, quietly smoking his pipe, he checks the starting prices to see what odds he's been given, and waits calmly until the net from the helicopter drops beside him on the slanting deck.

The net is winched up, taking the form of castellated battlements as it goes. Our hero knocks out his pipe on the battlements and advises, in his best Derrick Guyler voice: 'Get the strength of Anglers' Insurance around you . . .'

The He-man Angler

Word gets around the club. Big John's a-comin'. The bar goes deathly quiet. Nobody moves.

The door swings open. And in walks the biggest

'. . . but I like the men who do it.'

man north of the Severn, carrying on his shoulder a pair of wrenched-off lock gates. Dropping them on an incautious bailiff, he strings his built-cane rod like a longbow, fits a four-foot rod rest as an arrow, takes a long, slow, muscle-creaking aim and knocks the bung out of a barrel of Bass.

He fills a two-gallon bait can with the foaming brew and drains it dry with one gulp. Then he speaks:

'I gotta go now, folks. Big John's a-comin'.'

CHAPTER SIXTEEN

A Match For Any Man

Match fishing is the acme, the epitome, the essence, the peak, the zenith of fine coarse fishing.

The old-fashioned match angler is a gentleman in the truest sense, playing the game for its spirituality, its exacting tests of skill and cunning, its character-building qualities. He gives his opponents every chance, every benefit of every doubt. He is noble, generous, unselfish. A true sportsman.

All these qualities add up to one thing: failure.

With the increase in prize money, betting and cash from tackle firms for the endorsement of their products, match fishing is now Big Business. Because of this, the old sporting approach has become affected by business ethics and morality.

'Which,' as Gilhooley pointed out in a lecture to his Match-fishers' Mafia Summer School, 'would give yez all plenty o' scope if ye were not the foine upstandin' men that y'are.'

Gilhooley's lectures were designed to illustrate the corrupt and illegal practices which could lead to undeserved success in a match, and to act as an awful warning to anyone who considered using them. His pupils subsequently did very well, except for three who were caught at it.

With the maestro's permission, I am able to expose some of the more flagrant abuses of the matchfisher's code. Abuses that every right-thinking angler will condemn out of hand as unsporting, unBritish, immoral, dishonest, degrading, corrupting and useful.

Psychological Warfare

This can start well before a match and is concentrated on the main opposition: the reigning champion or hot favourite, and anybody else who is in the running.

If the champion is married, the campaign is made that much easier for the villain. About a fortnight before the match the post brings an envelope addressed to the champ. It is heavily scented and marked '*Personal and Urgent*'. Mrs Champ, being the normal kind of trusting, loving wife, will steam it open. Inside, written in red ink on mauve notepaper, will be the simple query:

'Darling,
Where *were* you last night?
Booboo'

If it were known that on any particular night the champ was out late, the message might read:

'Darling,
Thank you for the most marvellous evening. I can't wait for next Tuesday. Till then, Yogi my love.
Booboo.'

Tuesday night will be the weekly meeting of the champ's angling club social section, from which he invariably arrives home late and the worse for wear.

By the time Mrs Champ has finished with him, his casting arm will be in a pretty bad way. And about three days before the match, when Mrs Champ finds a pair of laddered tights in his overcoat pocket (slipped in as he stood at the bar, drinking kingsized scotches to help him figure it all out) his chances of even getting to the water will be slimmer than a skeleton on a crash diet.

It could happen, of course, that Mrs Champ does not open the letters or fails to spot the tights. In this event, the villain tries another tack. When the couple go out for a drink, he waits until Mr Champ has popped into the Gents. Then, in false beard and heavy spectacles, he walks across to Mrs Champ and says, 'Hello, love. Great to see you again. Is he still as frisky?'

As soon as Mrs Champ does the 'I've-never-seen-you-before-in-my-life' bit, the villain says, 'Oh, dear—I *am* sorry. You're not the one he was in with the other night. No, of course—she was blonde and a much younger lady. Oh, silly me. I'd better go before I cause any more trouble.'

This technique can work for both married and unmarried champs. As can the phone call from a female accomplice:

'Fred, I'm so glad I've been able to track you down. This is Doris. Doris—you remember. At the angling club dance last month. You don't? Well, you *were* a bit far gone. We went out to your car for a bit of . . . you know . . . And Fred, I'm ringing because something that should have happened hasn't happened. What do you mean, you don't know what I mean? I'm in the . . . I'm up the . . . I'm having a . . . Oh, Fred, I'm too worked up to go on talking to you. I'll get my solicitor to write . . .'

Another simple, but very effective, technique is the planting of rumour. Not *spreading* it, mind you. Just planting it. All the spreading will be done by friends of the accused.

Villain stands at the bar of champ's local and asks

the landlord, 'How is old Fred taking the inquiry,
then? Didn't you know? Well, perhaps it's not true.
I'd better not mention it. I'd be the last person in the
world to blacken a bloke's character. All right, if you
insist—but it's not come from me, mind. I heard it
from a bloke down at the club and he might have got
it all wrong. It's only that the committee are supposed to be looking into the draw at the last match.
Some of the lads reckon that Fred didn't get that peg
by accident. Know what I mean? Load of nonsense,
of course, with a bloke like Fred, but you know how
these things get about . . .'

Before you can say, 'Have you heard about Fred?'
the story has got around that he has rigged the draw,
used illegal bait, poisoned the swim, kept his finger

on the scales, embezzled the social fund and run off with the Secretary's wife.

A superstitious opponent is easy to demoralise. His superstitions are easily discovered over a friendly pint. Bad luck could be forecast by the sight of a black cat, a cross-eyed man, a bow-legged woman, a peacock's tail feather, a pair of boots on the table, or the sight of the new moon through glass.

The last one is easy to arrange, at the right time of the month, simply by saying, 'Like that, you mean?' and pointing through the pub window. And all the others can be fixed with varying degrees of effort and ingenuity.

Luck, of course, is very important to the superstitious angler. And villains have been known to arrange for lots of luck to be wished to a champion—by telephone, every half hour through the night before a match.

By the time the match comes along, the need for nobbling has grown even more urgent. Rigging the draw is not only reprehensible, but also very difficult. Angling club officials demonstrate a degree of incorruptibility which must get them waved straight through the Pearly Gates as soon as they have supervised their last weigh-in. Though there are several ways of rigging the draw, they are too well known to match officials to be of any practical use—including some methods of such sophistication that magistrates have heard their details in camera to avoid their popularity spreading too far.

So the nobblers have to stage their last attempts on the bank. It is possible, once the champion's peg is known, for odd bits of ironmongery—old bicycles, prams, milk crates, coils of barbed wire—to be dropped in his swim from the opposite bank by squads of junior Mafia hired specially for the occasion. This doesn't keep the fish away, but it doesn't do the master's tackle much good.

After that, apart from hiring these same mini-villains to pester the maestro during the match from as close as the stewards will allow them to get, the only other answer is for the nobbler to get drawn close enough to the champ to do it himself.

Remarks like, 'I really envy the way you can cast without getting snagged on those trees behind you,' or, 'I wish I could drop my bait dead-on like you can,' almost always ensure that he gets snagged on the next cast or drops his bait yards wide of the mark.

That, mind you, is almost legitimate gamesmanship compared with such tactics as hiding a bar of weighted soap in a ball of groundbait and lobbing it—quite accidentally, of course—into the champion's swim. Or carrying, in one's poacher's pockets, a set of waterfilled plastic bags, each holding half-a-dozen small roach or bleak which can be tipped into one's keepnet after a few pretences at striking and reeling in. Or slipping the odd spiral lead down the gullet of any fish which happens to have passed away during its stay in the net.

So strongly did Gilhooley feel about these abuses that each graduate of the Summer School took away with him, as a terrible reminder, half-a-dozen soap-filled balls of groundbait, a set of plastic bags with waterproof ties, and a range of spiral leads which could be hung from patent fasteners on the inside of a cuff and detached with a gentle tug.

And in their ears was ringing Gilhooley's final exhortation:

'Wid dese in front of yez, ye'll be remoinded of de umplumbable depths of morthal shame an' degradation dat some unhappy souls will sink to fer de sake of a few miserable pence. An' if ivver ye should need any more, ye'll foind de proices in de Black Museum section of me catalogue.'

CHAPTER SEVENTEEN

Game Fishing

As game fishing (fishing for salmon, trout and—if you're liberal minded—grayling) has still not disentangled itself completely from the dafter aspects of the British caste system, it might be as well to examine a couple of the basic myths about it before we go any further.

Myth One

There are those among us, brothers, who reckon that game fishing is strictly for the aristocracy, for the plutocrats, for the face-grinding capitalist exploiters of honest labour. That you need a pools win before you can even think about it. And that we don't want to know, anyway—that if the canal was good enough for our dads it's good enough for us.

A load of old shoemenders, brothers. Admittedly, if you want to fish the southern chalk rivers or any of the privately owned stretches of Scottish salmon rivers, you do need a pools win.

But there are lots of small rivers and streams which are full of trout and cost no more to fish than a coarse river. The growth of stillwater trout fishing on specially stocked reservoirs has increased enormously the number of waters. You can reach them now, brothers, because you've got a car, which was something your dads never had. Some of the bigger angling clubs have bought rights on some beautiful salmon and trout waters. You can go and fish those, brothers, and still have enough cash left for a bevvy.

Myth Two

That flay fishin', my deah fellah, is the only way to catch fish compatible with the dignity of an officer and a gentleman. And if you are a *real* purist, old chap, you must use the dray flay for trout and nothing else. That the only fish worth pursuing are the salmon and the trout. And that the skills of flay fishin' are infinitely superior to the chuck-and-chance-it methods of those roughnecks on the canal.

Balderdash, deah boy. Pish, tush, piffle and yah-boo sucks. Almost every fish has something to recommend it. And though dry fly fishing is an extremely beautiful art, every branch of angling has its own special skills.

The emergence of game fishing as an OK pastime came about as the Industrial Revolution got far enough under way to start killing off the fish in our rivers. As trout and salmon waters became fewer they tended naturally to become the province of the well-to-do. They tended also to be well away from the centres of population.

The situation was complicated further in the 1880s when Frederick Halford published his doctrine of dry fly fishing.[1] It was then very much a minority technique, used only on clear rivers and chalk streams.

It wasn't Fred's fault, really, that the idea caught on as it did, but soon he had a band of followers from the lunatic fringe. Before long the dry fly technique was being classed with fox huntin', pig stickin' and

[1] For students of the obvious, a dry fly is one which floats on the surface of the water, as opposed to a wet fly, which is fished below the surface.

170

Dervish bashin' as being one of the few sports fit for a gentleman.

The dry fly did, and does, work well on chalk streams and quiet, clear rivers. But soon it was being used all over the place on waters completely unsuited to it. The fact that those who used the dry fly on the wrong waters seldom caught anything didn't seem to be any deterrent.

A man using a wet fly was a boundah, an outsidah, a bolshevik, had no sense of duty, discipline or feelin' for the Empah. And as for those rough chaps who used worms and things—what could their nannies have been thinkin' of?

These attitudes have survived in some measure even into the Eighties, and it is still possible to get a great deal of social mileage out of dry fly fishing without actually doing any.

With a pair of cavalry twill trousers, a pair of chukka boots, a hacking jacket and a regimental tie (preferably from one of the more upstage regiments, and certainly not from any of the corps apart from the Armoured) one can mix with the other bluffers in the Angler's Rest and swing the lamp.

It is important to remember the vocabulary. *Fly*, for a start, is always *flay*. It's *fishin'*, not *fishing*. One talks about the *Mess* (omitting to mention that it was the Corporals') and never the *NAAFI*. It's the *Regiment*, never the *mob* or the *shower*. Now and again remember to say *don'tcha know* and *what, what*.

Any questions from the other bluffers about the fly you used to catch the mammoth trout you were telling them about can be answered with, 'A little thing I tied myself, actually. You know, a bit of game cock, a flash of silk thread, that sort of thing. Rather a monstrosity, actually, but it certainly pulled the little chaps in.'

In one's athletic days, one always played rugger, never soccer. And the scar on your forehead from a stray bottle in a NAAFI brawl in Famagusta is referred to casually as the old wound. ('Always acts up in the damp weather, old chap.')

The Cast

Fly casting is much more spectacular than bait casting. The line, instead of being gossamer-thin and practically invisible, is a tapered whiplash, heavy enough to be shot out under its own weight.

Instead of being sent out with one back and forward movement, this movement is repeated until enough line has been paid out to shoot the fly to its destination. This whip-waving action has been known to bring out the strangest reactions in the most unlikely people. After the banning of the courbash, it was no doubt a great source of comfort to many a retired colonial official.

First, we hold the rod in the right hand, with the thumb lying along the back of the butt, and pull off a few coils of line with the left hand. (For fly fishing a centre pin reel is always used). We switch the rod from side to side to let out a length of line about 1½ times the length of the rod, taking some more coils into the left hand to make up for it.

Now we swing the rod smartly into the vertical and a little to the right to send the line over our right shoulder. (Swinging the rod a little to the right saves having to take the fly out of the right nostril.)

When the line behind has reached its *full* extent, the rod is brought smartly forward. If the line has not reached its full extent, there will be a crack like a pistol shot to announce that the fly has snapped off. If, on the other hand, the line is not brought forward quickly enough there will be a soft flop on the grass to announce that the whole shoot has dropped to the ground.

When the line is fully extended in front, the coils in the left hand are fed through the rings. At the full extent of the forward cast, the line is brought back again over the shoulder. More coils are taken off the reel to be fed into the next forward cast.

When enough line has been let out, the rod tip is dropped as the fly reaches about three feet above the spot aimed at.

That's all there is to it. All you need to do it properly is patience, skill and about thirty years' practice.

There are variations of this basic overhead cast— the steeple cast, the backhand cast, the left hand cast, the side cast, the roll cast and the Spey cast—but you've got more than enough to be going on with.

Where to Start

If you want to practise your casting and at the same time get the feel of a trout, you could do worse than try it on a trout farm. It's not over-exciting, but you are certain of a catch.

The farms breed trout for stocking and for the city restaurants. Any spare trout, clapped out from breeding or too big to be edible, are put into a separate stock pond. They are so tame that they clamour at the surface for food every time anyone walks past the pond.

You can fish the ponds, for a quid or so, and with usually an upper limit of a brace of trout. The brace generally take all of a quarter of an hour to land, so on a time-money ratio it can be a dear do.

You will not be alone. The brisk, military-looking

A fascinating hobby . . .

man with tweed hat full of flies, who props up the private bar in the Angler's Rest, probably started his fly-fishing career on a trout farm. And will finish it there.

You'll see him in the middle of the pond, wading strongly, waving his rod like crazy and getting very angry with anyone on the bank who casts within twenty yards of him. His technique is obviously too sophisticated for the simple, tame trout, because it generally takes him all day to catch his brace. He will be using a Black Gnat or a Wickham's Fancy on fish which are more used to fighting over a bucket of high protein pellets.

Fly Tying

Fly tying is a fascinating hobby which has kept some anglers happy for a lifetime and put others in a padded cell within a fortnight.

There are so many different flies that the only instruction possible, in a book of this size and level of ignorance, is on how to tie a basic fly.

The basic kit is quite simple. You need a vice. (You probably have one already, but this is the dreary kind used for holding the hook.) Then you need some hackle pliers for plying the hackle. Then some scissors, wax, wire, tinsel, varnish, beeswax, silks, red wool and an assortment of peacock's tail feathers, gamecock hackles, mallard's wing feathers, red ibis feathers, partridge tail feathers, red seal's fur, a moleskin and a pair of hare's ears. (I kid you not. Nauseating, isn't it?)

With the addition of some bat's bumfluff, under-arm hair from a horned toad and some dried skin from the navel of a sunpeeled maiden, you have an ideal all-purpose kit for Hallowe'en Night.

Let us take the making of a typical, basic fly. You start by fixing the hook in the vice, just above the barb. Rub a length of silk with beeswax, lay the loose end along the shank of the hook then wind the rest of it up to the eye and back. Getting this bit right should not take more than two or three days.

Now we tie on some hackles for the whisks (the sticky-up bits near the eye of the hook). Lay them along the shank and wind the silk round the ends near the eye. Then lift up the whisks and wind the silk underneath them so that they stay up. Rub some moleskin between your fingers and then rub it round the tying silk so that it sticks to it. Wind on the tying silk and you have a revoltingly fat moleskin dubbing body.

Now you can take a big hackle, or a piece from an old fur stole or passing cat, lay it along the shank and wind the silk round it at spaced intervals, so that the hackle fibres stick out.

You can tie on a tail of more hackles, more stole or more cat, and there you have it—Dougal, from Magic Roundabout.

The Grayling

The grayling appears between the trout and the salmon because the poor old thing is the odd one out. She is a member of the salmon family, but prefers to spawn with the coarse fish. This lack of discrimination means that up-market game fishermen curl their lip at her.

She is a very beautiful fish—one of her nicknames is the Lady of the Stream—and is supposed to smell of thyme. She has a very small mouth, the mark of a real lady. You can almost imagine her saying 'prunes and prisms'.

Salmon Fishing

If you can afford it, the great thing here is to go the whole hog and hire a gillie. This is a morose Scottish bloke whose job it is to take you to the salmon lie and help you to get your fly or spinner under its nose. It is always prudent to tip him first. It won't bring a smile to his face, but it might result in a bigger salmon than the starveling he had in mind for you.

A gillie is a very patient and respectful man who will call you 'sir' and give a string of instructions on casting and on playing the fish. If you lose a hooked salmon, however, his patience will evaporate and he may so far forget himself as to call you a stupit, spotty faced, knockitty-kneed Sassenach loon. This

176

temporary loss of control, known as Gillie's Freakies, can be cured by beating him over the head with a five-pound note.

The odd thing about salmon fishing is that, as far as bait goes, it is much more democratic than trout fishing. You can use whopping great wet flies, which are generally more hook than feather, sprat · dead-baits, prawns, spinners and even bunches of worms.

Salmon bite out of temper, not out of hunger—they don't feed on their way up from the sea. Hooking him, however, is the beginning of your problems, not the end of them. He will make for broken water, he will pull like a fifteen-stone Channel swimmer, he will sulk at the bottom and refuse to budge.

Sidestrain should turn him from the broken water. If it doesn't you will have to shell out for a new rod tip. You can move him out of a sulk by pulling him across the current. This exposes his flank to the push of the water and throws him off balance. Or it throws you off balance and exposes *your* flank to the push of the water. Happenings such as this are another reason why gillies prefer to be tipped in advance.[2]

There is another style of salmon fishing which in the past has saved many a Prussian princeling from

---

[2] A sulking salmon which suddenly stopped sulking was responsible for the demise of Sir Parsifal Goldstein, the Manchester plastic submarine manufacturer. His gillie, Mr Hamish MacMuckle, told the coroner: 'His last worrds tae me, sorr, as he wis sweppit doon the burrn, worr: "Hamish, ma old an' faithful retainer o' many yearrs standin'—Hamish, ma wallet is yourrs." '

This claim was not pursued after another witness had testified that (a) Hamish was known in the gillying fraternity as the Strathclyde Stiffener, (b) that it was Sir Parsifal's first time out with him, and (c) that Sir Parsifal's last words were simply 'Gurgle, gurgle'.

shame and mortification, and which is now used extensively by visiting Midlands property developers and second-hand car tycoons. The gillie hooks the salmon, brings it to the bank breathing its last, then hands the rod to the client with a tug of the sporran and says, 'now, sorr—you bring him in.' As the angler stands there, wondering what the hell he is supposed to do, the gillie leaps into the water with a four-foot gaff and yanks the expiring salmon on to the bank.

'Ah, sorr, ye played him like the gentleman that y'are,' says the gillie. That's generally good for another tenner.

CHAPTER EIGHTEEN

Sea Fishing

One of the myths of our island race is that we feel, periodically and irresistibly, the call of the sea. When we get back from a trip on a heaving boat, we realise that most of our ancestors must have walked here before the Channel was cut.

What we mistake for the call of the sea is the euphoria of ozone, winkles and Guinness which overcomes most of us during our week in Blackpool; that feeling of superhuman well-being which can be used either to boost the birthrate of the following spring or diverted towards the pursuit of the saltwater monsters. Most of our wives, with the kids already squawking for ice creams, buckets and spades, candy floss and a donkey ride, would much rather we got with the monsters.

The first thing to do is to get kitted out. Tartan shirt, windproof trousers, canvas jacket with kinky rope fastening, jaunty trawlerman's cap guaranteed to make anyone but a genuine jaunty trawlerman look a right burke, and a pair of bright yellow wellies.

Once the wife sees you in that lot you have no chance at all of getting to work on the birthrate. You are now left with a choice of fishing from the beach or the pier, from the rocks, from a rowing boat or—in company with a bunch of other yellow-wellied euphorics—from a hired inshore fishing boat.

Reading the Shoreline

The tide comes in and goes out twice a day. The best

time of all to fish from the shore is high tide, which generally happens a couple of hours before you get up or a couple of hours after you've gone to bed.

Low tide gives you the chance to study the shoreline, so that you will know where the fish will be when the sea comes in. You look for channels in the sand or between rocks, hollows in the sand, undercut cliffs, sewage outfalls, groups of isolated rocks and clumps of weed. The fish coming in on the tide will be found in or around all of these places. The big snag is that, when the tide does come in, it covers all of these landmarks up and you can't for the life of you remember where they were. Still, it's fun.

The Tide

Once-a-year anglers tend to forget that the tide doesn't just come straight in up the beach. It creeps up channels, sneaks around the back of sand-banks and rock outcrops, fills in hollows with incredible speed. Anyone turning round to wave to the wife and finding that most of the Gulf Stream is between him and dry land, can do one of three things: wade, swim for it, or shout, in a dignified manner, 'HAAAAAAAAAALP!!!!'

Anglers who, through lack of experience, fail to recognise the outward and visible signs of a rising tide, are often made aware of it by a cold, damp feeling in the wellies, evidence of sudden saltwater corrosion of the fly-zip or, in extreme cases, a chill feeling under the armpits accompanied by a strange floating sensation.

Baits

All sea baits have one thing in common: they're revolting.

The most widely-used sea baits are lugworms and

ragworms. You can catch them by digging at low tide where you see their holes on the surface of the sand.

Lugworms are found about nine inches below the surface. More correctly, they *live* about nine inches below the surface, but burrow like the clappers at the first hint of disturbance and thereafter need a drilling rig to locate them.

Ragworms live nearer the surface in muddy areas and again dislike being disturbed.

Unless you enjoy digging great pits all over the beach for the possible reward of the tail end of a

. . . no chance at all of getting to work on the birthrate

sleepy lug, it's best to buy the worms from professional bait diggers. Their prices are one of the contributory factors towards the seaside inflationary spiral, but if you jolly them along with some merry repartee, they might even give you a few fresh worms mixed in with yesterday's leftovers.

It's quite easy to tell if the worms are fresh. If the lugs just lie there, all squashy-looking and smelling like a skunk on heat, they're yesterday's. If a ragworm bites you, it's today's.

Octopus, squid and cuttlefish can be used, either as chunks or cut into strips. Again, it's easy to tell how fresh they are. If you can get within three feet of them, they're fresh.

Crabs, shrimps and prawns can be used live. With prawns and shrimps the hook is pushed carefully through the tail. After which the hook is pulled carefully out of the finger. Small crabs are used whole, with the hook pushed through the shell from the back and out between the eyes. They don't like it. Boiled shrimps and prawns can be used, with a sprinkle of paprika or a dab of tartare sauce.

Shellfish—mussels, razor fish, whelks, limpets and cockles—can be used once you've got them out of the shell. Limpets display a great reluctance to let go of their rock, and the more you bash them the tighter they cling. The best technique is to turn your back on them, whistle a few bars of soothing music (*Greensleeves, In A Monastery Garden, Bless This House*), then turn round quickly and give them a swift sideways karate chop. After you have come out of the First Aid Room you should have no difficulty in getting them out of their shells.

Mussels tend to come off the hook easily. This can be overcome by tying them on with a piece of wool. Bits of brightly coloured wool also attract fish. Any difficulty in keeping the wool on the hook can be overcome by tying it on with a piece of mussel.

Bits of fish or strips of fish skin are very useful baits and not nearly so smelly as some of the alternatives. Seaside branches of MacFisheries do very well out of it.

Almost anything else sufficiently nauseating can be used as a sea bait: raw meat, offal, boiled macaroni, bacon skin, strips of kipper and bits of old sock soaked in pilchard oil.

There is a fair selection of artificial lures made specially for sea fishing, but almost any freshwater artificial lure—spoons, plugs, spinners and wet flies—will work. Or not, as the case may be. Anyway, it gives you a chance to use up all the monstrosities you made at home.

Most casual sea anglers forget to include a bag of groundbait among their tackle. A good all-purpose groundbait is a collection of bread, macaroni, minced meat, offal, crushed crab, chopped lug and rag, fish guts and chopped up bits of fish. All this is mixed together into one irresistible *pot pourri* with pilchard or cod liver oil. You will now appreciate why most casual sea anglers forget the groundbait.

Shore and Pier Fishing

Shore and pier fishing, although the most convenient form for anglers, have the highest spectator accident rate. Statistics for the summer of 1980 show that, of the total number of injured spectators:

15 per cent were either hooked or laid out by a weight on the back cast

7.5 per cent suffered damage to either nostril from a poke from a rod tip as the angler bent down to retrieve his catch

13 per cent slipped on baits or fish guts left on the pier

12 per cent were passing swimmers who were hooked and reeled in before the mistake was discovered

8 per cent were occupants of rubber dinghies, floating mattresses or inflatable Donald Ducks, which were punctured by hooks on the reel-in

10 per cent were amateur motorboat pilots who went under the part of the pier marked 'Danger—fishing in progress—no boats allowed'

34.5 per cent were small boys discovered messing about with anglers' catch, bait or tackle. Injuries were mainly paired cases of mild concussion, a result of scrubby little heads being banged together, or incipient cauliflower ear.

Casualties among anglers, apart from the usual hookings, poisonings, bites, stings and brainings with four-ounce leads, were mainly attributable to injuries received from large men who slipped on their baits during constitutionals along the pier.

From a pier one can fish by paternoster, leger or float. The paternoster is the method most favoured, on the mistaken premise that the more hooks there are, the more fish will be caught. In practice, it means that there are more hooks to get snagged on the piles and stuck into old ladies.

Leger has the disadvantage of being carried by the current into every possible snag. The constant vigilance makes it a method not highly favoured by contemplative anglers who like to tie their rod to the rail and keep in touch by extra-sensory perception from the pier-end bar. Flatfish angling by leger also has the drawback of attracting hordes of crabs. An old dodge is to fix a small cork above the hook to keep it above the notice of the crabs. This also ensures that it is kept above the notice of the flatfish.

Float fishing means that the angler has constantly to be at the rail, keeping an eye open for the bob of the float or for a drift towards the pier supports. This constant and active participation is not what pier fishing is all about.

As soon as the bar at the pier end opens, 93.4 per cent of all anglers lash their tackle to the rail, clip a bell on the end of the rod and adjourn for just a quick one. Four hours later they roll out and are dreadfully disappointed to find that not only have they not got a fish, but that their bait has gone as well. ('Ey oop, our Albert—that must have been a big bugger. Look—'e's 'ad me bait clean away. Wait till I tell our Ida . . .')

Some of the keener types stand by the bar window to keep an eye on their rods in case the tip suddenly bends to a record-breaking conger. (It's no use just listening for your bell. Every bell on the pier is tinkling away like crazy in the wind, fish or no fish.) But the keenness of the voyeurs doesn't last more than a couple of pints. After that they settle down out of the draught for some serious drinking.

Surf fishing from the shore is a very skilful way of taking fish, especially bass, and one which accounts for most of the swimmers hooked during any given season. Its very skilfulness, however, accounts for its relative lack of popularity.

Rock fishing gives the angler a chance of real isolation, especially if he is fishing on a rising tide and neglecting to look behind him.

Groundbait can be laid all the way up the rock so that, as the tide rises, it is washed off to attract the incoming fish. The angler will find much to study as he stands, solitary, on his rock. And much more if he steps on any of the groundbait. He will find, for instance, that British coastal waters are much colder than they look, and that even sea anemones are not so pretty viewed from six feet under. The same opportunity for close study of marine life is given to anyone who leaps gaily from one weed-covered rock to another, or who steps back to admire his catch.

Should the rock angler be cut off by water too deep for conventional wading, and can see nobody on the shore behind whose attention he can attract, he must strip off completely, wrap his wallet and any other valuables in a plastic bag and tie this to the top of his head. He can then wade, chest high, or swim back to the shore.

At his emergence on to the beach, covered only in a rather becoming outfit of blue goosepimples, he will become aware the presence of all the people who weren't there before. Including a policeman who will book him for doing naughty things, shivering suggestively in the presence of female persons, indecently exposing his goosepimples and wearing a plastic bag on top of his head.

Rowing Boat Fishing

Fishing from a rowing boat is one of the really rugged pleasures of sea angling. All alone, you can driftline at anchor for mackerel, bass, cod, pollack, coalfish, garfish and bream. You can weigh anchor and drift with the tide, fishing sink-and-draw with feathers for mackerel. Then you can look up and wonder where the shore has gone to. Not only that—which direction was it in when it went?

Losing direction out of sight of shore is a real danger, especially on an ebb tide. It is some consolation if you have your passport with you, and

enough money to pay your fare back from Norway, Denmark, Sweden, Holland, Belgium, France or Spain. If funds are low or getting back is a matter of some urgency, however, you must take immediate action.

Remember the direction finding methods you used in the Boy Scouts. Check the nearest tree to find which side the moss grows on. Or point one hand of your wristwatch at the sun, the other at your left knee, and divide the space in between. This should point either to the North or South, the East or West, depending on the time of the year.

Having found your position, row for a bit, steadily, and sing hearty sea shanties to keep up your spirits. Then tie your vest to an oar, wave it, and scream in a confident tone.

The dangers of boat fishing can be minimised by observing a few sensible precautions. As in rock fishing, never step back to admire your catch; do not dance or light fires while the boat is in motion. Give way to ocean liners and atomic submarines. Do not throw stones at albatrosses, or shout rude words at them. Before you leave harbour, put a mark on the side of the boat to show which way North is.

If the boat is holed, or a sudden rainstorm breaks, you will recognise the fact by the way the boat fills with water. You will also be pleasantly surprised at the speed you can row.

Communal Boat Fishing

For the gregarious angler, fishing with a party of kindred spirits from a hired fishing boat is a great delight. You need not worry about tackle or bait; the skipper will supply that. Concentrate on loading yourself with as many bottles of the hard stuff as you can comfortably carry and on getting a place at the stern of the boat. (The stern is the blunt bit at the back. The wisdom of getting a place there will become apparent later on.)

The skipper heads out to the nearest fishing mark and gives the signal for the lines to be cast out. Your companions are cheerful and ruddy cheeked, glowing with sea air and good fellowship, and giving out with lusty choruses of 'Way-ay, up she rises!'

The first fishing mark is always a formality. There are never any fish around. So the skipper orders the rods inboard and sets off for another mark a couple of miles further out. Here the water is noticeably choppier and the boat pitching a bit more. Out go the rods. This time there is little singing; a mood of introspection has settled over the jolly band.

In the absence of any bites, the rods are hauled in again and the boat sets off to a third mark. By now the sea is much fiercer and there is a small gale blowing.

At the third mark the lines are heaved out by men whose complexions have taken on a curiously greenish cast, and whose free hands are clutching at their midriffs.

One by one, they drop their rods and hang desperately over the side of the boat. After ten minutes or so of making agonised noises, they collapse one by one into the scuppers and lie there, groaning gently and mouthing phrases like: 'Must have been barmy,' 'Bugger this for a game of soldiers,' and 'If I get out of this in one piece I'll never belt the wife again'.

You, meanwhile, at the back of the boat, are bearing the pitching and rolling with fortitude, fighting off the nausea with the hard stuff, and possibly even catching fish. You now realise the advantages of fishing from the back of the boat, which is probably anchored or drifting with its head into the wind. The anglers in the middle of the boat are being covered in spray, both from the sea and from the anglers in the bow. The anglers in the bow are soaked to the skin. Along both sides of the boat is a tangle of abandoned lines.

In the stern you are safe. Because of the boat's shape, all the spray and unwanted breakfasts fly harmlessly past. And your line is carried away from the boat, well clear of the tangles on both sides.

After a couple of hours of pitching, rolling, yawing and whatever else boats do in the circumstances, the skipper casts an experienced and pitiless eye over the bodies in the scuppers and shouts 'Right, lads, we're going home'. All the groaning, writhing anglers, who by now have long given up any pretence of enjoying the trip, will heave a sigh of relief and wash down more Kwels with heavily-laced tea.

It is customary at this point for some wag to announce that, if there's anything in you, the sea will bring it out. It is also customary for this wag to be beaten over the head with the nearest ling, pollack or codling, or to have a live conger stuffed down his trousers.

Some Interesting Sea Fish

Apart from the dangers from wind and tide, sea and storm, hook and weight, there are also dangers in sea fishing from the catch itself. Sea fish are not at all keen on being caught and have their own special ways of showing it.

The angler learns very quickly, for instance, not to go 'Koochy, koochy, koo', to the pretty little whiting. The pretty little whiting has a set of teeth which turn the chin-chucking accompaniment into 'Koochy, koochy—aaaaaaaargh!!!' And anybody daft enough to try the same thing on a ling is known thereafter to his friends as Lefty.

Careless conger fishermen can be recognised by the way they walk up to the bar, shout 'Four pints, please' and hold up two widely separated fingers. It is still common, even after centuries of sweeping up finger-ends littering the bottoms of boats, for a conger to be slung into a box along with the rest of the catch. Before long, someone prods around in the box for a mackerel to cut up as bait. As soon as his exploring fingers come within chomping distance of the uptight conger, he realises that his ambition of becoming a concert pianist has hit a snag.

Trouble with a conger starts as soon as it is hauled inboard. It twists and turns, bucks, somersaults, spins, loops, thrashes and writhes. All the time its mouth is snapping like the scissors of a demented barber. Half Nelsons, full Nelsons, Japanese strangleholds and Indian deathlocks are not recommended as a means of subduing it unless you are on the short list for a job as harem master.

The only sure way to deal with a big one is to gaff it with two gaffs—one at the head and one at the tail—bash it on the tail to keep it quiet, and then cut through its spinal cord, just behind the head, with a sharp knife. Yuck.

Be careful with the knife. Don't lunge. If ever you see a party of anglers trooping off a boat, carrying one of their number and singing

> *Hi Ho!*
> *Hi Ho!*
> *Old Fred has lost a toe . . .*

you can lay even money that Fred was a lunger.

The conger is then dropped in a bag, the trace cut, and the bag tied tightly at the neck. ('Rubbish! No need at all to cut the trace. Just unhook the conger as you would any other fish,' he said, prodding me with his stump.)

The poor old thing, gaffed, bashed, knifed and tied up in a sack, should now be past caring. But after lying quiet for a couple of hours, waiting for the string to work loose, many a conger has slipped out for a quick chomp at the nearest wellie.

The weever is a nice little thing. Covered in poisonous spines. One jab from these spines can put you straight into hospital. Every seaside hospital ward has one—the bloke who knew all about the weever, but who insisted on stamping on one with plimsolls or rope-soled sandals.

The skin of the lesser spotted dogfish was once used as sandpaper. Lots of anglers who never knew this interesting fact before are acquainted with it after trying to hold a spinning dog in their bare hands. Another interesting discovery can be the spines in front of the dorsal fins of the spur dog. Excellent for blood poisoning. Giving it to you, that is.

The torpedo ray isn't caught very often. When it is, it can be recognised by the electric shock it gives. 'That,' you can say knowingly to the bloke who has been thrown half-way across the boat by the charge, 'is a torpedo ray.'

The thornback ray and common skate have neat little rows of thorns all the way down their tails. Which is why it it is not a pleasant experience to handle them. The tail of the sting ray is even better equipped with a barbed and poisonous spear. Never attempt to hold its tail while you take the hook out: ask the chap next to you to do it.

The poor old skate is the one to feel sorry for. The male skate has a pair of 'claspers' on its underside, like the two blades of a pair of shears. These claspers, when they come together, can do a neat pinking job on your hand, and many fishermen are in the habit of cutting them off as soon as the fish is caught. This is a bit anti-social, really, because the claspers are the sex organ of the male skate. I mean, how would *they* like it?

The claspers have given rise to a variation on the old hedgehog joke:

Question: How do skates make love?

Answer: Very, very carefully.

One jolly thing about all sea fish is that any bite, cut or jab from them is poisonous and liable to turn septic if not disinfected very quickly.

Anyone for fishing?